PUBLISHING FOR IMPACT

PUBLISHING
FOR IMPACT

DAWN DUKE
PAM DENICOLO
ERIN HENSLEE

$SAGE

Los Angeles | London | New Delhi
Singapore | Washington DC | Melbourne

⑤SAGE

Los Angeles | London | New Delhi
Singapore | Washington DC | Melbourne

SAGE Publications Ltd
1 Oliver's Yard
55 City Road
London EC1Y 1SP

SAGE Publications Inc.
2455 Teller Road
Thousand Oaks, California 91320

SAGE Publications India Pvt Ltd
B 1/I 1 Mohan Cooperative Industrial Area
Mathura Road
New Delhi 110 044

SAGE Publications Asia-Pacific Pte Ltd
3 Church Street
#10-04 Samsung Hub
Singapore 049483

Editor: Jai Seaman
Editorial Assistant: Lauren Jacobs
Production Editor: Manmeet Kaur Tura
Copyeditor: Sarah Bury
Proofreader: Jill Birch
Marketing Manager: Susheel Gokarakonda
Cover Design: Shaun Mercier
Typeset by: C&M Digitals (P) Ltd, Chennai, India

Library of Congress Control Number: 2019944358

British Library Cataloguing in Publication data

A catalogue record for this book is available from
the British Library

ISBN 978-1-5264-6510-8 (HB)
ISBN 978-1-5264-6509-2 (pbk)

Dedication

We dedicate this book to all researchers out there diligently writing their research for a range of different audiences so that their findings and ideas can make a difference to academic thought in their field, and to the world. It is especially for those new and experienced writers who have shared with us in workshops and at conferences the challenges they have faced and their solutions, their moments of despondency and delight, so that they and others might improve their practice.

Last but not least, we dedicate this book to our wonderful, supportive families, who have patiently encouraged us throughout this project and our careers. Thank you, Steve, Callum and Maya Clowes; Vincent Denicolo; Billy, Lizzy and Liam Henslee.

Contents

List of further resources

Activities

Examples

Figures

Information boxes

Reflection points

Table

Top tips

Voice of experience

About the authors

Dawn Duke is the Head of Researcher Development and Engagement within the University of Surrey's Doctoral College. She leads the team that supports the transferable/employability skills of postgraduate researchers and early career researchers across all disciplines, as well as delivers supervisor training. Dawn received her neuroscience PhD from Imperial College. In 2008, she moved from researching and teaching neuroscience to concentrate fully on researcher development. She has worked to embed and normalise skills training to better prepare researchers for the variety of opportunities available to them. Through her work at Surrey and a partial secondment as Director of Graduate Training for the Southeast Physics Network (SEPnet), she has focused on bringing researchers together with employers from a range of sectors, integrating this wider range of expertise into training, creating spaces for discussion and experience sharing. Dawn believes that the world would be a better place if the amazing research that is done within our universities had an even greater impact on policy, society and the economy, and is dedicated to enabling the next generation of researchers to take on this challenge. Dawn met Pam through a mutual friend at University of Surrey, and they soon became not only colleagues but also good friends. Dawn is published in both the fields of neuroscience and higher education and has experience writing in a variety of formats, including journal articles, book chapters, books, lay articles and blogs. She has now joined Pam as an editor on the Sage book series *Success in Research*.

Pam Denicolo is an Emeritus Professor at the University of Reading, a chartered constructivist psychologist and honorary pharmacist, who provides consultancy on doctoral support and research methodology as well as examining doctorates in institutions worldwide. Previously she established, managed and developed the University of Reading Graduate School, providing a substantial contribution to its Research Methods, Generic Skills and Doctoral Supervisor training. Her passion for supporting graduate students and other early career researchers is demonstrated through her numerous successful doctoral candidates and examinees and her leading roles in national and international organisations such as the International Study Association on Teachers and Teaching, the Society for Research into Higher Education Postgraduate Network, the RCUK Impact and Evaluation Group, several working groups of Vitae including the development of the Researcher Development Framework (RDF), the QAA Doctoral Characteristics Advisory Group, and the UK Council for Graduate Education, all of which have resulted in many publications, presentations and workshops. Through these organisations she met up with Julie and Dawn, who became inspirational collaborators on many projects as well as valued friends. Pam provides consultancy and workshops worldwide on doctoral issues. She edits and contributes to the Sage book series *Success in Research*, which is aimed at those in the early years of a research career, and co-edits and co-authors with former doctoral researchers a series with Brill/Sense dealing with *Critical Issues in the Future of Learning and Teaching*.

Erin Henslee has BSc degrees from Virginia Tech in Engineering Science & Mechanics and Mathematics, where she then worked as the undergraduate recruiter for the College of Engineering. During this time, she also completed an MSc in biomedical engineering. Erin then moved to the UK where she completed her PhD in Biomedical Engineering at the University of Surrey in 2016. She also enjoyed coordinating undergraduate labs for the department of Mechanical Engineering Sciences. Her PhD work led to a BBSRC funded post-doc in circadian electrophysiology of red blood cells. In 2016, Erin left the lab to join the Researcher Development Programme, where she worked in Dawn's team at the University of Surrey supporting other researchers on their doctoral journeys. In 2018, she moved back to the USA to become part of the founding faculty for the Department of Engineering at Wake Forest University. At the crossroads in her post-doc life she realised she wanted a career involved, in some way, with support, inclusion and promotion of STEMM. She remains dedicated to doing just that. Erin has always been a discipline crosser and has experience in interdisciplinary publication in a variety of genres, including 4* journals.

Acknowledgements

We three authors thank every researcher who has ever attended one of our training sessions or talks, and who has generously imparted their ideas. We are grateful to everyone who has shared their thoughts, comments, concerns and fears about all aspects of publication with us and who has, we confess, contributed covertly to this book. Without you, we would have little to say.

We also owe a special debt of gratitude to Dr Michael Rose, Dr Kate Turner, Dr Patrick Brindle, Dr Christian Gilliam, Dr Christine Daoutis, Dr Montserrat Rodriguez-Marquez and Dr Alex Pavey, who contributed specialist chapters.

We would also like to thank all the anonymous people and experienced writers who contributed 'voices of experience', whose advice and knowledge will help many others. We are especially grateful to the following people for their expert views, honest reflections and words of wisdom:

Dr Lucy Bell, Senior Lecturer in Spanish and Translation Studies, University of Surrey

Prof Pam Burnard, Arts, Creativities and Education, University of Cambridge

Dr Alice Motes, Research Data and Preservation Manager, University of Surrey

Prof David Sampson, Vice Provost, Research and Innovation, University of Surrey

Dr James Suckling, Environmental Sustainability Research Fellow, University of Surrey

Dr Esther van Raamsdonk, Post-doctoral researcher, QMUL and Oxford

Special acknowledgments go to our collaborative authors (and co-conspirators) in the *Success in Research* series: Julie Reeves, Susan Brooks, Sam Hopkins, Marcela Acuna-Rivera, Carol Spencely, Sue Starbuck and Alison Yeung, with an extra special thanks to Alison for her superb editing.

A very special thank you to all our family and friends, and colleagues at SAGE, who have kept us going while we wrote this book, and others in the series.

Prologue: Who will benefit from this book and how?

Who is this book for?

Publishing has always been a defining characteristic of an academic role; even before the printing press was invented, scholars put quill tip to paper. Yet publishing in academe today is very different, not simply because of changes in the physical process of writing, but because the rationale for doing so has expanded and diversified, encompassing a wider population within universities and research institutions.

This book was written to serve that whole wider population. Further, it was inspired by the increasing need to communicate with a broader audience than was previously considered appropriate. Newer and established academics, as well as postgraduate, doctoral and post-doctoral researchers, and **third space professionals** – those people whose work comprises elements of both professional and academic activity (Whitchurch, 2008) – not only benefit from sharing ideas and research with each other, but now need to demonstrate the value of their research and enterprise activities to a range of stakeholders and potential beneficiaries. If you are one of these groups, then we hope you will find this book helpful in your authoring endeavours.

We have deliberately included the word 'impact' in our title to capture our intent to help you produce written work that will be effective both in reaching and influencing your chosen audiences and in contributing to the Impact Agenda that pervades higher education (Denicolo, 2013). While those who work in education always have hoped that their vocations would serve useful purpose, that value to society nowadays needs to be evidenced in some tangible form. It has to be seen to be contributing something of consequence, producing impact. To do that, other people need to know about what you have done, why and how, and what it means for them.

What is unique about this book?

We are alert to the fact that there is a multitude of books dealing with how to write (anything) effectively and/or elegantly, and shelves full of books on how to get published as an academic. In this book, not only do we combine advice on both of those activities, but we seek to add something extra, which responds to the current need for those in academe to convey the impact of research both within and outside academia. While the traditional mode of conveying impact through the medium of journal articles is effective within academia, it is not so for other professionals in society, policy makers, commerce, industry and the general public, who are unlikely to acquire or read those sources. Therefore, those within academe now need to have honed skills in communicating the impact of their research in ways that are both accessible and attractive to those professionals as well as in ways expected within academia.

This book, then, aims to provide guidance on designing an appropriate publication strategy for reaching out both within and beyond academe. Included is advice on how to prepare written material for journal articles and for a range of other media. It draws on the multiple perspectives of others, writers experienced in a range of media and publication activities, to complement the diverse aims and range of individual backgrounds and purposes of potential audiences.

How can you make best use of this book?

With the breadth of readership of this book in mind, we have divided the chapters into three parts. Part I focuses on the complex planning that needs to be engaged with as a foundation for successful publication. Chapter 1 explores how to create a publication strategy suitable for your personal research niche, while Chapter 2 considers the different types of audiences you may be seeking to engage with, and how that influences your mode of communication. Chapter 3 addresses how to benefit from the peer review process, and highlights the way in which that process, when used well, can increase your chances of publication success and build your confidence. Part I concludes, in Chapter 4, with the important process of planning your writing, including guidance on how to find time to write and how to overcome challenges to writing.

Part II deals in depth with the variety of writing outputs that you may need to consider from high-impact journals in Chapter 5, book and chapter writing in Chapter 6, a monograph derived from your thesis in Chapter 7, to writing intended for lay audiences in Chapter 8. Each chapter deals with the process involved in writing for a specific audience, addressing such issues as style and voice. The principal aim of Part II is to demonstrate the importance of adapting your writing for the specific genre and your particular audience in order to effectively communicate the impact of your work.

Having emphasised the importance of tailoring your writing for both medium and audience, Part III considers how to promote your manuscript to gain the best impact. Chapter 9 explains the relatively new and complex world of Open Research and how to navigate it. The focus of Chapter 10 is on how you can make sure that your publication is seen, read and acted upon by as many people as possible. In the chapter, we propose a range of methods for promoting your publication. Reflecting on the Impact Agenda, Chapter 11 delves into how your research can make impact beyond academia to influence policy, society, culture and the economy through strategic publication and promotion of your research outputs. Finally, in Chapter 12, we hope to inspire you, as a published researcher, to take control of the measurement of your impact by demonstrating and demystifying evidence for it in various forms.

If you are new to publishing your research, then you might well find it useful to read quickly through the whole book to get a feel for the whole process, then to work through each chapter as that topic becomes pertinent to your writing and publication stage. If you have some writing experience already, then you might select specific chapters to extend your ideas or to stimulate new ones. In order to help both types of reader, we have attempted to follow a process model but have incorporated some signposts to other chapters throughout where issues are elaborated on or viewed from a different perspective. We have also deliberately included some repetition so that you need not be page turning back and forth too often.

How can this book help you?

This book includes information, explanation and clarification of the many facets of publishing you will encounter as a researcher but, importantly, it also encourages you to engage with the process. Thus, although the text includes, for instance, Information Boxes and Voices of Experience, it also incorporates Activities, Reflection Points and Top Tips, drawing on writers', readers' and publishers' experience, in accessible, interactive form to help you, the reader, be actively participating and productive. We also provide 'Further Reading' at the end of chapters so that you can follow up any references we draw on and any other reading that has proven useful to us and our colleague researchers.

Voice and vocabulary

We have, as part of our commitment to engaging with you, attempted to write this book as a conversation with you as a colleague. Several authors have contributed to the writing of chapters, adding to them and editing them. Further, we have drawn on expertise throughout our networks to bring in different perspectives, ideas and resources. Thus, you may well discern multiple voices, each with its own accent, despite our valiant attempts to edit the book into a cohesive whole. Since we make a point of emphasising the need to beware of jargon and of the different nuances of meaning each brings to what seem to be common words as well as the arcane ones of academe, we have also provided a glossary. This is not a dictionary but is, rather, a guide to how we have used words in this text. We hope that the different viewpoints and accents make the book enjoyable as a collegiate conversation as well as informative.

Further reading

Denicolo, P.M. (2013) *Success in Research: Achieving Impact in Research*. London: SAGE.

Whitchurch, C. (2008) Shifting identities and blurring boundaries: the emergence of Third Space professionals in UK higher education. *Higher Education Quarterly*, 62(4): 377–396.

PART I
Planning for success

1

How can you create a publication strategy?

In this chapter you will:

- Examine the various reasons for publication
- Explore various forms of publication
- Think about how to make publication choices and plans
- Create your own publication strategy
- Discover how planning and producing a varied publication portfolio can enhance your career

The purpose of publication

Why do we publish? Of course, we all know that publication is a measure of academic success. The phrase 'publish or perish' is well used within academic circles. People fret over quantity and **star rating** of publications and which of these two is the most important, with the latter pulling ahead in **success measures** in recent times. It is easy to focus on these metrics and academic pressures when thinking of the motivations for publishing. However, there is a deeper reason for publishing. Publication is about sharing your research and your ideas with others.

Research that is not used to inspire further research and academic thought in the field is as good as lost. Ideas that are not shared to create agreement and controversy, to generate new questions or to change our views are not fulfilling their full potential. Publication is a vehicle to reach out beyond ourselves and indeed beyond those within our tight circles to communicate with the broader world.

Publication moves the world of research forward and is a vehicle for research to influence policy and to benefit society, economy and culture.

The rapid technological advances of the last decade, which have brought considerable opportunities for the global communication of research, are changing the nature of research and academic publication. There is now a huge diversity of audiences with whom to share our precious data and interpretations. At the same time, these audiences are being bombarded with more information than ever before, making it ever more difficult for any individual publication to stand out. This is compounded by the new publication requirements from funders and the increased use of metrics by higher education institutions and international league tables, making publication decisions increasingly complex.

In this chapter, we consider how you can navigate this new publication landscape. We focus on the importance of publication in terms of information and idea sharing and propose that a strategy based on this will serve any researcher well throughout their evolving career. First, we consider the different forms of publication.

Different types of publication

Academic publication

There are several types of standard academic publication formats with conventions varying by discipline. Because of this variation, it is important for any newer researcher to learn from at least one senior mentor in the field when grappling with early publishing decisions. In this book, we aim simply to alert you to possibilities and new ideas about publishing, which you will then need to translate into your own disciplinary context.

In general, peer-reviewed journal article publishing is the standard and most reputation-enhancing way to publish in the majority of disciplines. When considering publishing journal articles, it is important to consider the reputation and audience of the journal (see Chapter 5) and to understand the peer-review process of that journal (see Chapter 3). Journal articles most commonly focus on research results; however, there are journals that also include, or even specialise in, review articles or methodological/methods/theory papers, either solely or additionally.

In science disciplines, journal articles tend to be the predominant medium for communicating research; however, there are some fields where papers presented at specific conferences compete with them for prestige. For example, in computing and some engineering disciplines, such as Electrical and Electronic

Engineering, conference publications are held in very high esteem. For these disciplines, knowing the key conferences and understanding the peer-review and publication process involved is extremely important. Even though some disciplines might not attribute as much prestige to conference papers as those cited above, in general, conference papers are still an extremely valuable medium for building your research reputations for all disciplines. Making your name known by presenting in front of your research community is critically important advertising for your work and for enhancing your professional standing (see Chapter 10).

While journal articles remain important in many arts, humanities and social sciences disciplines, books and book chapters are also common and prestigious. Books made up of a collection of academic chapters written by key people within a discipline are common in some social science disciplines, and it can be a sign of professional esteem to be invited to contribute. Whether deciding to contribute a book chapter to a book or to undertake the coordination of a book project yourself, decisions regarding publishers and access to the book will be important to the eventual impact of the publication (see Chapter 6).

In the arts and humanities, the monograph continues to hold its high standing in academic publishing. The first monograph a researcher writes is often based on their doctoral **thesis**. Although the thesis is usually written by the time of proposing the monograph to a publisher, the story then needs to be crafted into this new style, making the monograph a substantial work in its own right (see Chapter 7).

Before reading further, it will be useful to identify the custom and practice of your own discipline area. We ask some questions to guide you in Reflection Point 1.1.

Reflection Point 1.1

Identifying prevailing publication outlets in your field

Thinking about the research literature you have been reading, what format is most common in your discipline? When writing, which journals contain the articles that you cite the most? Who publishes the books to which you frequently refer?

Non-academic publication

There are more options for non-academic publishing than ever before. Whereas traditionally academics had quite a limited reach beyond their academic bubble, today the options perhaps seem limitless and at times overwhelming. Anyone can reach a huge international audience within seconds on **social media** platforms, and books can be published independently and put online for all to read. Whereas research was once confined to its ivory towers of the world, the gates are now open to a world eager for real evidence-based information. Knowing how to utilise this power in a way that promotes research and engages your target audience is the real challenge. Questions that arise include:

- Which avenues are best?
- What are the potential problems and pitfalls you need to be wary of?
- What choices should you make?
- When might it be useful to use non-traditional pathways?

The most traditional forms of non-academic or semi-academic publication are educational books, either like this one – targeting professionals and practitioners – or **textbooks** targeting students. These types of publication are well-established options, and can be very satisfying avenues for publication (as your authors can attest). When thinking about undertaking such a book, it is important to recognise the time commitment this will take and to make sure you find the right publisher for you and your project. You will have to put in a book proposal that will be peer-reviewed.

Different publishers will have various specialist areas, and so it is important for you to be aware that if your book idea does not match the publisher's niche, it is unlikely to go any further. You should also make sure that the eventual book will be accessible to the audience you wish to target. It is also useful to discuss with publishers early in your decision-making process about how much they anticipate the book selling for, and what their main method of distribution is – are they selling directly to customers or selling to university libraries or both? There is also the option of self-publication. Although this option can ensure the book is quickly and openly available, if this is what you wish, it will lack the production and marketing support as well as the credibility that a good publisher brings to a project. (See Chapter 6 for more details on publishers and how to choose and use them.)

Academics have also long been involved in publishing policy documents and publishing through the media. These outlets can be excellent pathways to take research findings directly to different key audiences. When thinking about how research eventually gains impact, often a first step is a publication or other type of communication that bridges the academic world and a specific outside audience – a professional group, for instance – that can make use of the findings.

Today there are even more ways in which you can quickly and freely communicate and engage openly with different audiences about your research. For example, you can use social media, create a website or a **blog** or even put together online learning material. For the latter, you may wish to apply for a **creative commons licence** (https://creativecommons.org/licenses/) for your material, as this gives you a recognised copyright but still allows open access usage of the material you create (see Chapter 9).

The above options are just a few of the many currently available, with the number increasing at an unprecedented rate. If you are a newer researcher, it is important to learn quickly how to evaluate the various options and make smart decisions about what type of non-academic publication/communication you may wish to invest time and energy in. We discuss these options in greater depth in Chapters 10 and 11, but here you might find Reflection Point 1.2 useful in helping you to evaluate non-academic sources.

Reflection Point 1.2

Considering and evaluating your own use of non-academic media

Do you read work written by academics in any non-academic form? Do you read blogs? Are you on **Twitter**? What draws your attention to research published in these forms? How is it different from reading academic work? What use do you make of it?

Other outputs

Although this book is focused on publishing, it is worth noting that not all impactful outputs are in the form of the written word. Depending on your academic discipline, you may produce compositions, datasets, patents, gene sequences, computer code, and so on – the list continues to grow. All these outputs are important to developing your professional profile and your research niche(s) (see Part III for more discussion on these various impactful outputs). Therefore, you should ensure your publication record reflects the whole of your output portfolio and serves to advertise to a range of audiences the various lines of impact your research has and could have. Keeping all of this in mind, it becomes evident that a good publication strategy is important to ensure your work is having the greatest impact possible. To make a start on that task, engage with Activity 1.1.

Activity 1.1

Learning from the experts – part 1

Think of two academics in your field that you admire. Look up their academic profiles on their webpages. Conduct an author literature search on each using Google Scholar or a discipline-relevant publications database such as ERIC, PsychInfo, PubMed or Web of Science. Then also do a non-academic Google search of them. What does their full publication profile look like? Where do they publish their research? In what format? Do they blog or tweet about their research? Do they write for the media or other lay public publications? How different are these two academics in terms of their publishing profile?

Make notes about the potential avenues for your publication future, thinking of ways in which you could emulate those academics.

Your aims, key messages and intended audience

The first step to any good strategy is to look at the big picture and think about what you intend the eventual outcome to be. Your publication strategy must reflect what you wish to be known for as a researcher and as a professional, which is a major consideration irrespective of whether you intend to make your career totally in academia or in commerce, industry or the professions. Important elements of your renown are the ideas and skills that make you unique and the precise area(s) where you wish to contribute.

Your publication aims can fall within a wide range of different categories: to disseminate research findings; to share advances in research approaches; to conceptualise new ideas and theory based on a review of published work; to inform practice; to educate; or to engage a wider audience. To create a good publication strategy, you should think about incorporating several of these different aims, explicitly thinking about how to differentiate yourself from your supervisor, or other academics in your discipline area, to create a unique publication profile. Again, a good way to start this process is to be guided by other academics you admire using Activity 1.2.

Activity 1.2

Learning from the experts – part 2

Using the two academics that you picked for the first activity, skim over their publication list and their public profile. What appear to be their main niche areas of research? What are the main ideas and approaches they have been building up in their publication record? Look back through their publication history and decide whether these have changed and evolved over time. Do they promote these messages outside the academic context?

Voice of Experience 1.1

Different publication streams

My research was stimulated by a desire to find ways of improving how abstract ideas in science could be communicated to learners and to the general public. As an erstwhile scientist and a practising psychologist, I explored different ways of conducting such research and found a special approach with a range of techniques that enabled access to other people's different ways of viewing the world.

Over time, during and considerably more so beyond my doctorate, my writing began to be dominated by wishing to improve teaching and learning and to use those techniques to explore alternative realities in a range of professional arenas. Despite pressures to write internal and national policy documents competing with academic publication, mainly related to the implementation and elaboration of the research approach and methods, I developed an additional passion for writing to improve professional practice beyond formal education. Table 1.1 shows how the topic areas became distributed over time in the course of my academic career.

Table 1.1 An academic lifetime of writing by topic and distribution

Decade	Psychology	Research Methods	Teaching and Learning	Professional Development
1984–90* (Postgraduate researcher > Lecturer)	8	6	5	6
1990s (Reader, Course leader, Director of Research)	10	1	14	10
2000s (Professor, Centre Director)	6	5	12	12
2010s to date (Emerita, Consultant)	4	4	6	21

*1985 Also produced a doctoral thesis that combined aspects of all categories.

These publications include extensive documentation (e.g. for University or government or professional bodies), journal articles, books and chapters in books, ordered under area of substantive content. Thus, they targeted different types of audience. They do not include the writing of research proposals but do include the results of successful research funding and support from professional societies.

At first it was a struggle to research, write and teach as well as bring up a family, but I found that having a variety of topics to write about fitted in with the time-space I could carve out, spurred on by whichever passion predominated at that time. Soon I was responding as much to requests as to strategic career need, but in later years I have been able to write what I want to write when I want to. Indeed, I seem to hardly know how to stop writing. There is always something I am impelled to put finger to keyboard to express.

A Professor Emerita

As a newer researcher you may not be able to do all of this at once, but developing a strategy will serve you well in the long term. Create the vision first and then a plan that will get you there over the years. This vision depends first and foremost on your intended message, what you want passionately to say, and then who may be interested in, and influenced by, your message.

Thinking about your audience for each message is a supremely important task. Often people naturally picture their audience as very similar to themselves. In this case, you may be thinking of your audience as researchers who are in a similar discipline to you, perhaps using a similar research approach to you and caring about the same research problems that you do. No doubt, people like this are an audience for your publications. They most definitely will read your work. This group of people is relatively small, though, and usually consists of your collaborators or your competitors. These people will read your work no matter where or how you publish it. If you are looking to increase the impact of your publications, you should be looking to expand this readership. In other words, as you have the attention of the 'will reads' already, you need to focus your efforts on the 'might reads'. To do this, you should think creatively about who *might* read your work and who could be better informed or could practise more effectively if they did.

Getting the people who *might* read your work to become the people who *do* read your work is the key to an impactful publication. The 'might reads' are a large and diverse group of people, but because they are not doing exactly the same research as you, it is important to think about the specific interest of this group and tailor your publication to reach them. Activity 1.3 will help you discover different audiences who might be interested in your research.

Activity 1.3

Finding your 'might reads'

Brainstorm and draft out your 'might reads'. Start with people closer to you, perhaps people in your discipline area but using different approaches, people using similar approaches but in a different discipline. Now think more broadly: perhaps people in other disciplines or possibly people in certain related professions. Write down every potential audience for your publication without forming any judgements until you have a good list of different types of people who make up your 'might reads'.

Once you have identified people who might be interested in your publications, you can start thinking about how to tailor your message and your writing style to reach them. One strategy for doing this is to write your papers for a broader audience and publish them in places that reach this broad audience. Journals have different defined readerships and target audiences; some are very niche while others are quite broad (for example, an education journal, a higher education journal or a journal for doctoral education and training). The journal's website will specify their target audience, which can help you decide whether this is the best home for your publication and how you should adapt your message to fit with the journal. Articles that have greater downloads and citations tend to be those that attract many 'might reads', often attracting readers from a broader disciplinary base by having key messages that appeal to different types of reader (see Chapter 5).

Attracting a broad readership to one specific publication by publishing in a journal with a diverse readership is one way to engage more people with your publications. However, it may be that within your list of 'might reads' there are some people who are unlikely all to read the same types of publication. In this case, another strategy for attracting your 'might reads' is to consider multiple publications tailored specifically for these different audiences. This will allow you to present your research in a variety of argument/presentation styles appropriate for the different audiences.

Adopting this multiple publication strategy is particularly useful for some interdisciplinary work, where two distinct disciplines would be interested in different aspects of your research. In this scenario, you should look at tailoring and then publishing two different works, one in each of the respective discipline journals. For example, a researcher who looks at the use of music within the classroom may want to publish research with details about the music composition in a music journal; results regarding learning outcomes in an education journal; and explanations of creative research **methods** in a journal focused on qualitative methodology. You might even wish to publish in a professional educators' magazine, bringing your research directly to the practitioners who could make use of it.

Interdisciplinary research, such as the example above, can lead to a wide range of publication opportunities; however, there can also be unique challenges to publishing this type of research. This is particularly true when your research falls in-between the remit of different journals, making editors concerned that their audience will not be interested in the content of your paper. The Voice of Experience 1.2 gives insight into strategies developed by two academics involved in **interdisciplinary research** to overcome these challenges and to capitalise on the diversity that interest boundary-crossing research can have.

Voice of Experience 1.2

Advice from interdisciplinary researchers

Voice one

Getting interdisciplinary research published certainly has its challenges. In a way, it's much more difficult than publishing within your own well-defined discipline, where you know what your readers want, and the material you submit will cohere with reviewers' expectations. Yet it also opens lots of new doors for exciting research publications: a wider range of journals to choose from, broader readerships, and so on.

Here are my top tips for publishing interdisciplinary research, based on my experience to date:

Choose your target journals carefully. Don't just read the Aims and Scope of journals on their home pages. Read articles from that journal, but also check out the editorial board carefully. If that journal only has representatives from one or two fields, it is unlikely to publish articles that fall outside these disciplinary boundaries. If the journal is genuinely interdisciplinary, its editorial board members should come from a range of different disciplinary backgrounds.

Frame your research clearly. As interdisciplinary as your research is, you still need to locate it in a specific area of research. If you are publishing in a Cultural Studies journal, for example, make sure that you frame your research through Cultural Studies debates, concepts and theory – even if your research draws from, and/or contributes to, a much wider array of disciplines and subfields.

Be patient and don't give up! It may take longer to get your interdisciplinary work published in a journal – it requires a bit of experimentation and is more hit-and-miss. However, the rewards are great, and it's worth the wait.

Lucy Bell, Senior Lecturer in Spanish and Translation Studies

Voice Two

Creativity and innovation thrive in the synergistic interactions within interdisciplinary research in both the arts and sciences. In addition, the arts can offer a context for high-performance teamwork, change management, intercultural communication, improved observational skills and adaptability, as highly valued employability aspects. My own work in interdisciplinary research strategies has been exemplified in the boundary-crossing involved in 'STEAM education research', with its addition of 'arts' to STEM subjects.

Anglo-centric literature currently predominates, partly as a result of the language medium adopted by international research journals, and partly due to the cultural roots of STEM, with which STEAM is often associated. Either way, getting published in research journals requires that you become familiar with and engage with diverse groups of key stakeholders from different levels and sectors of education, both nationally and internationally, to widen your **critique** and understanding of the potential of interdisciplinary research. The frames used for interrogating interdisciplinary literatures needs careful thinking followed by development of new analysis procedures for researching interdisciplinary practices.

The key idea here is that in the combining of two or more academic disciplines, which leads to surfacing new conceptions of knowledge (epistemological stance), the assumptions upon which different ways of knowing are engaged and legitimised (ontological stance), and the nature of their relationships (ethical stance), that the rigour, contribution and originality of interdisciplinary research requires the creation of interdisciplinary (new) tools, understandings and expertise to design and customise the research. Interdisciplinary research methodologies and methods link and integrate theoretical frameworks across disciplines.

Getting familiar with several interdisciplinary research journals offers a great starting point for meeting up with interdisciplinary research teams who will share different disciplinary collaborations within a single scientific culture, crossing cultural boundaries.

Pam Burnard, Professor of Arts, Creativities and Education

Pam recognises and thanks the British Educational Research Association for their support in funding the Research Commission and all participants who contributed to the dialogues leading to the final report. The resources developed by the Commission are archived at https://steam research.wordpress.com. For further examples of interdisciplinary projects see Further reading at the end of this chapter.

As with the previous example, it is not uncommon that some of your potential audience lies outside academia. Reaching such lay audiences often requires publication beyond the bounds of normal academic publishing. For example, perhaps you research 'Neglected Tropical Diseases', so you would want to publish your research findings in a biomedical journal to move the science forward. You may also want to target people who make policy, or even the general public, to raise awareness and support for these lesser known and funded diseases, requiring a different type of publication. The power of lay publication should not be underestimated. These types of publication can be your avenue to make a real impact on social/cultural and economic issues. They also can attract attention and extra readership to your academic publications, bringing in new 'might reads' who were previously unaware of your research. See Chapter 2 for more discussion on how best to attract different audiences to your publications and your research work.

Creating your publication strategy

Now that you have thought about your publication aims and messages as well as the different audiences you may like to reach, it is time to put together your strategy. A senior colleague once advised that you should always have at least one publication in each of these three publication stages at any one time:

1. A publication that you are planning, i.e. doing the research on currently, or writing, or planning a book proposal for, etc.
2. A publication that you are writing.
3. A publication that is in the process of being published, i.e. submitted and undergoing peer-review, corrections or is in press.

This may seem ambitious if you are at the start of your career, but once you get your publication strategy into action, this is something you should aim for. In fact, when you are further on in your career, it is perfectly possible to have multiple publications in each of these three categories. Moreover, at the beginning of your writing career, thinking about heavily loading the number of publications you have in the planning stage is advantageous, because not all publications will completely get through the three stages. Indeed, those publications that make it to Stage 3 may well be pushed back to Stage 1 as a result of the peer-review process (see Chapter 3). With this in mind, within your publication strategy, you should include a contingency for publications being rejected at the peer-review stage. This should not necessarily be seen as a totally negative outcome (although we admit rejection is never fun). It provides you with insight into the requirements (some of them arcane) of specific journals as well as providing valuable **feedback** for improvement from reviewers. All of this can make your eventually accepted publication better.

Choice of journal

It is also important to stretch the potential of your research to be in journals with a broader and bigger readership, attracting more 'might reads'. Publication in these higher-impact journals is competitive. It could be that, if you are getting all your publications accepted on first submission, then you are not aiming for high enough quality journals. Depending on your field, a 25–50% rejection rate is probably desirable to ensure that you are aiming for high enough quality journals (see Chapter 5). A strategy with a pipeline of planned publications helps to reduce the chance of your publication profile drying up for any long period of time.

Content priorities

In putting together your publication strategy, it is important to identify your top priorities. In general, this should be publishing your main research results and ensuring that these are accessible to the widest audience likely to read and cite these publications (see Chapter 9 to learn more about openly available publication options). Therefore, add this to your strategy, first thinking about how long it is likely to take to get the research completed and to a point where you can write your publication, as well as thinking about how and where you would like to publish. Next, you can think about other publications that you may be able to write before and/or after this. Is there a need for a review article in your field or a methodological paper? Are there other types of lay publication that you want to pursue? When would be the best time for you to write these?

Authorship

Another option to consider is collaborative publishing. **Collaboration** is a great way to increase your publication profile, reducing your overall effort and adding in a large dose of motivation because you do not have to do it all on your own. Not all your publications have to feature you as the primary author; second authorships, or middle authorships are advantageous as well. Importantly, collaborations, particularly international collaborations, often lead to more highly cited papers, and can increase your professional reputation. It is important to choose collaborators carefully. You need people with integrity, who are reliable and who complement your own expertise. Of course, this means that you must also be a positive collaborative partner. The authors of the *Success in Research* series can all attest to how collaborative writing can lead to publications that are much richer in content than would have been possible by any one of us alone. We certainly have found the experience of co-writing with colleagues to be an inspiring and fulfilling experience. See *Success in Research: Inspiring Collaboration and Engagement* (Reeves et al., 2020) to learn more about establishing successful research collaborations.

Defining success

The final point to consider for a good publication strategy is how to know if your strategy has been successful. You have defined key messages and identified the target audiences you are trying to reach. You have thought about the format of your publication, that is, journal article, book chapter, and so on. You have thought about the best location for the publication in terms of the specific journals you wish to target, publishers you want to work with or websites you would like to blog on, etc. But how will you know your strategy has been successful? To be able to reflect on the relative success or not of your publication strategy, it is helpful to have some success measures identified within the strategy itself.

Getting a paper accepted can be one measure of success, but you will also want to have measures of people reading your publications and using them. In Chapter 12 we identify a variety of ways you can determine the impact of your publications. These measures can help you continually modify your publication strategy so that you are better able to communicate with your intended audiences.

You should now have all the information you need to start to put together your own unique publication strategy. Top Tips 1.1 provides a summary of advice to help.

Top Tips 1.1

Ten publication strategy tips

1. Determine the key messages you would like to convey.
2. Think about the different types of people who may be interested in your messages.
3. Prioritise publication of your research results, and take the time to ensure their quality and fit with the identified publication type and location.
4. Plan different types of publication, including both academic publication and lay publication; you can maximise your impact by generating a varied publication portfolio.
5. Take advantage of opportunities to co-author publications.
6. Plan for peer-review rejections, using them as learning experiences.
7. Aim high in terms of journal and publisher quality but have pragmatic second and third options.
8. Actively promote your publications (see Chapter 10).
9. Define success measures within your strategy, reflect on how successful your publications are and adapt your strategy to continually improve (see Chapter 12).
10. Enjoy the process. Your passion and care for your work should shine through in all of your publications.

By filling in the template in Activity 1.4, you will start to make your publication strategy concrete.

Activity 1.4

Creating your publication strategy

Fill in each of the boxes, to bring together your publication strategy. Make sure you frequently reflect on your plan and make adjustments to ensure it is realistic. Also do include success measures, perhaps considering the information in Chapter 12. This will allow you to better reflect on whether your plan is having the impact you intend. Also think about how you will promote each publication (see Chapter 10).

Your Publication Strategy				
1. Key Messages/ Ideas you want to be known for	2. Potential Audiences	3. Types of Publication (include format/ location e.g. book/SAGE, blog/ Wordpress, etc.)	4. Promotion Routes	5. Prioritisation (most important for your career)
		6. Action Plan (include objectives, time frames and success measures)		

We encourage you to think of this initial draft of your publication strategy, created through Activity 1.4, as a draft version that you can revisit as you go through this book. In the next chapter we will explore how best to communicate with specific target audiences, and the following chapter will provide more detail about the peer review process. These two chapters will inspire greater reflection on Boxes 2 and 3 of your publication strategy. Chapter 4 will help you to take this strategy forward by making a realistic plan, which will better enable you to complete Box 6. In Part II, you can then start looking in more detail at how you can accomplish specific publication targets within your publication strategy, while Part III will enable you to focus on ensuring that you get the most benefit possible from your publications.

Finally, it is important to realise that this strategy should continue to be revisited from time to time as you grow and change as a researcher, which we all do throughout our careers. There should also be reflection on what has worked well within your strategy and what has worked less well. Thus, there should also be some flexibility both to improve your strategy and to take advantage of new and unplanned publications opportunities that come your way.

Further reading

Becker, L. and Denicolo, P. (2012) *Success in Research: Publishing Journal Articles.* London: SAGE.

Reeves, J., Starbuck, S. and Yeung, A. (2020) *Success in Research: Inspiring Collaboration and Engagement.* London: SAGE.

SAGE Publishers (n.d.) *How to Get Your Journal Article Published: An Online Guide by SAGE Publishers,* https://journals.sagepub.com/pb-assets/PDF/Author%20 Gateway%20PDF/N8J1907%20-%20How%20to%20get%20published%20 Author%20Gateway_FINAL.pdf (last accessed 23/04/2019).

Terras, M. (2014) Want to be taken seriously as scholar in the humanities? Publish a monograph. *The Guardian Blog,* www.theguardian.com/higher-education-network/blog/2014/sep/30/publishing-humanities-monograph-open-access.

Tullu, M.S. and Karande, S. (2018) Success in publishing: selecting an appropriate journal and braving the peer-review process. *Journal of Postgraduate Medicine,* 64(1): 1–4.

Wager, E. (2016) *Getting Research Published: An A to Z of Publication Strategy* (3rd edition). Boca Raton, FL: Taylor & Francis Group.

2

How do I attract different audiences to my publications?

Guest author: Michael D. Rose

In this chapter, you will be encouraged to:

- Think more about your range of audiences – from those who 'will read' to those who 'might read' – and how you can turn the latter into the former
- Reflect on the benefits and challenges of different types of journals and books
- Consider what will grasp different audiences, beyond simple questions of style or terminology
- Explore the potential of different kinds of collaboration

Identifying different readers

We talked briefly in Chapter 1 about identifying the 'might reads' as well as the 'will reads' within your research audience. As we emphasised earlier, turning 'might reads' into 'will reads' by strategically publishing and shaping your work can dramatically increase your reach and boost your profile. This is the theme of this chapter. Diversification of this kind can also be an asset to you as a researcher, teaching you to write in different styles, appreciate new perspectives on your own work, build up new and useful contacts, and increase the potential impact of your research.

As discussed in Chapter 1, a helpful approach is to consider your own specific 'niche' within academia: what do you want to be known for, what ideas inspire you and spur on your research? This does not mean confining yourself to one tiny corner of academia – far from it – but identifying your potential specialisms and interests can help you to build a strategy for future work. It is usually better to aim for a spread of different publications, rather than simply a large quantity: this maximises your potential readership and also allows you to rework material to fit the angle or interest of each type of publication.

We start by considering the variety of what is available within your academic field, before broadening out to other connections you can build. You can think of your research as having a spread of audiences: do you focus on reaching other specialists in your field, or the full range of people potentially interested in it? The former is likely to have more direct and immediate connection to your work but can be a limited and fairly static audience; the latter has enormous potential but needs good judgement and communications skills to make an impact. Further, the former will be looking for detail and will be familiar with your technical vocabulary; the latter will value guidance about points of general interest written in a jargon-free style. We will consider such issues in the next sections. Planning your publication profile to cover a combination of in-depth and wider-spread areas gives you the most options over the longer term. Often you can target key points at which the interests of these groups meet. Figure 2.1 illustrates where different types of audiences might overlap, and how you might balance your writing to fit the anticipated reader; consider making your own graphic when planning your next piece. One factor to attend to is the different types of publication you will work on, which we will turn to next, starting with journals.

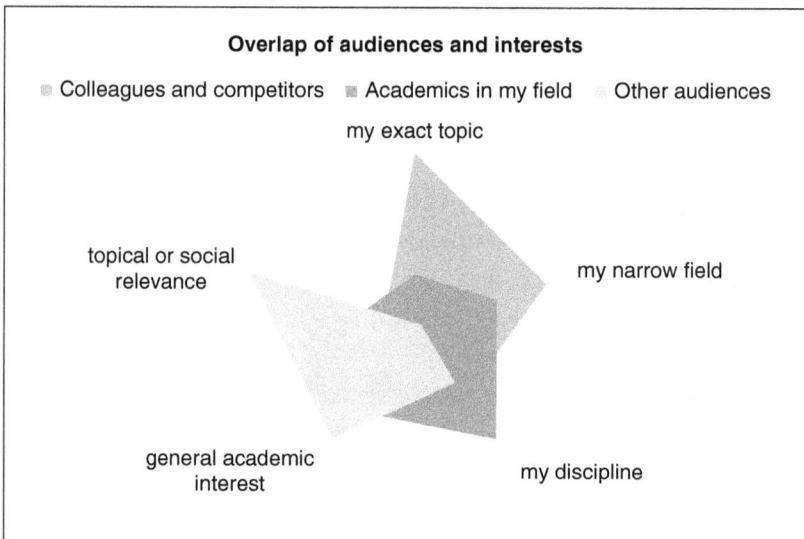

Overlap of audiences and interests

Colleagues and competitors   Academics in my field   Other audiences

my exact topic

topical or social relevance

my narrow field

general academic interest

my discipline

Figure 2.1 Where do my audiences overlap?

Journals

You will know from your own research which journals are the highest-profile, commonly called **Four Star journals**, writing for which is discussed in Chapter 5. Their editorial demands are a recognised marker of quality. Aim high when choosing your ideal publisher, especially with material that is at the core of your research. However, especially for the top-rank journals, some realism is needed too. Steel yourself for disappointments and have a back-up target if your first choice is not possible; take advice from experienced colleagues about where and when to submit. It is important to balance quantity with quality, since to publish regularly is both necessary and a significant achievement, but you do not want to 'waste' your best research on an 'easier' publication that will not be as widely noticed. Intelligent planning of your publication strategy should allow you to mix-and-match different levels and types of publication. Each of these audiences demand different kinds of writing, and we are going to explore some examples.

You will no doubt be familiar with very specialist journals of great interest and value, but only to a limited scholarly community. These constitute your 'will read' audience, where you can go into the scholastic minutiae of your topic, assured of an engaged and highly knowledgeable response. Your writing here can be highly technical and assume considerable foreknowledge; it will need to be precise and stake a careful claim to its original contribution. It will also need to be well founded in the current literature, about which you must demonstrate great familiarity. This can be simultaneously the most comfortable and the most nerve-wracking kind of writing, since you are bound to have an engaged (and possibly passionate) readership who are, by profession, also going to be intensely critical; there is nowhere to hide. Counterintuitively, although this kind of writing is designed to be objective and exact, it can feel the most personal, since you have worked so hard to craft every nuance and check every reference, date and figure.

In addition to knowing your 'home turf', make sure you have an overview of journals that cover your immediate field, and beyond that, the discipline more generally. Although there will still be clear reasons why your research will fit into these journals – and will appeal to the 'will reads' – be mindful of your purpose in submitting a specific article, which may include also attracting 'might reads'. For these you will need to provide more background knowledge germane to your research and make more of a case for its relevance to the targeted scholarly community. Avoid writing in a way that would exclude a more generalist reader (for example, by being too technical or too narrowly focused) and consider how your project links with current trends in the discipline. For example, watch out for announcements of special editions of journals on a topic, or current ideas that are generating a lot of interest. Perhaps what you argue about one author can be applicable to others, or the experimental framework you have developed can be adapted to another setting.

A further level of publications will mostly connect with 'might' readers, covering very large areas of your field (e.g. *Nature* in the sciences or *Essays in Criticism* for literature, languages and culture). Here again, you should bear in mind both your intended audience and your intended outcomes. Make sure you have familiarised yourself with the journal's style (language, length, referencing, figures) and that you pitch the information at a suitably broad, but professional, level. For example, the advice to authors for *Nature* includes the following:

> The journals are read mainly by professional scientists, so authors can avoid unnecessary simplification or didactic definitions. However, many readers are outside the immediate discipline of the author(s), so clarity of expression is needed to achieve the goal of comprehensibility. (www.nature.com/authors/author_resources/how_write.html)

'Might' readers will need to be captured quickly, since their interest will be provisional, and potentially fleeting. Also consider that for international journals many readers will have English as their second language, so avoid colloquial or unnecessarily elaborate expressions. The key is to have a title and abstract that are accessible and that explain the 'why' and the 'so what' of your research. An inclusive title that clearly indicates the content or issue – rather than an exclusive one that will only appear significant to those with an existing grasp of your topic or technical considerations – will be much more attractive. Also remember that search engines will find your publication more often if your key terms are in the title.

Within the article itself, the focus and the possible implications should be stated from the beginning. Eventually the data or argument will have to speak for themselves, but give them the best chance of being heard by inviting readers in.

Your intended outcome should be part of your larger publication strategy and will include which readers you want to capture. Voice of Experience 2.1 shares the reflections of a colleague on her relevant publishing experience.

Voice of Experience 2.1

Building your network through publication

Publishing in different places can have a hugely positive impact on your network. My first article was a small discovery on the main author I worked on in my thesis:

John Milton. This article was not full-length, but it announced to a broad audience what I was working on. From there, I targeted the major specific journals with an audience of 'will reads', such as the *Milton Quarterly*. The responses I received to these publications were highly specialist, and also highly informative. The positive reception gave me then the confidence to pitch more widely, submitting to the *Seventeenth Century* and *Renaissance Studies* journals, focusing not so much on Milton, but on my transnationalist method. In one of these cases I gained many advantages through a collaborative submission. I wrote a journal on travel diaries together with a scholar whose research concentrates on Dutch texts rather than English. We pooled our resources and increased the radius of our interested readers to include researchers into both nations, as well as showing how what we were each doing could be complementary and providing a model of transnational research in action. My next step is a forthcoming article in a journal that publishes articles on any aspect of literature, allowing me to reach audiences outside my author-interest field and historical period.

I have found that conferences are a brilliant way to create challenging opportunities to move outside my immediate research area. This has facilitated publication of my research in rather unexpected contexts and has forced me to find connections with areas that might not strike me at first as overlapping. For example, I went to a conference on 'War and Peace' that included all periods and in all aspects. I presented quite a broad paper on the seventeenth century. There I met another academic working on similar ideas but in different time periods. We later wrote an article together that combined both our expertise, leading to new findings, and new readerships, published in a journal I might not otherwise have considered.

Dr Esther van Raamsdonk, Post-doctoral researcher

It is important to remember that most journals will have a range of different types of content, not just full articles. Reviews can also establish your position by the way you situate and assess the work done by others. Do not feel too restricted to your specific field in accepting review commissions, since you will be able to comment interestingly on work being done in related areas, too. Shorter pieces, such as 'rapid communications', 'notes and queries' or 'letters', can be great places to report quickly on a new discovery or to make a smaller point of interest. Although often targeted at discussions within a quite limited sphere, these pieces are short enough to be accessible to others and can be a useful invitation for collaboration.

Sometimes your judgement can be guided by which route to publication will have the greatest impact. This can include how high-profile the journal is, the width or importance of the intended audience, as well as how different publications complement each other as part of your profile. Measuring impact after the fact can be tricky, since you are competing with many other voices in a crowded field. In Chapter 11 we will look at **bibliometrics** and **altmetrics** as ways of measuring and strategising impact.

Altmetrics can be a particularly interesting way of thinking about how and where to publish, since they illustrate better than citation counts the fact that publication is a two-way process. Naturally you are aiming to secure an interested audience in your core knowledge, and specialist publications will focus on this. Capturing more diffuse audiences can be an introduction to your research, but has the additional potential of directing readers to your more detailed publications in turn. In Reflection Point 2.1, we invite you to think about where you might target different kinds of publication, and the pathways that will lead new readers back to you.

Reflection Point 2.1

Key journals

What are the key journals in your field? Are you publishing and planning across the full spectrum? Have you considered your potential audiences? Think where your 'might reads' will go for their information, and the keywords they may search by. What will lead them from there to your core research?

Collaboration

One excellent way to increase your spread of audiences is through collaboration and it is common in most disciplines, although the number of collaborators will vary according to discipline. As a general rule of thumb, in biosciences 30+ authors is not unusual, while in the humanities more than two authors is quite rare. Where you are reporting on a larger project, it might simply be the only way to acknowledge all those involved. There are natural benefits to writing collaboratively, including sharing the workload and necessary expertise, and increasing the likelihood of reaching new audiences, especially if you are working with someone who is more established. You just need to be aware of how working with multiple contributors can slow the writing process down as multiple revisions are often required, and that you might need to manage some differences of opinion along the way.

For this chapter we concentrate on the possibilities for collaborating with someone outside your immediate project or discipline. This can naturally feel like more of a jump into the unknown but can repay your efforts with a new perspective or unexpected connections. Perhaps an interpretivist perspective can enrich and contextualise austere positivist data, or a method developed for a psychological investigation can be applied in the classroom. Increasingly, interdisciplinary work is finding an interested audience, and can give a concrete demonstration of how your work can be influential in other areas. However, be prepared to face some challenges alongside these opportunities, as described in the Voice of Experience 1.2 in Chapter 1.

As with writing for different journals, writing an interdisciplinary piece is not simply a matter of altering your writing style or level of detail. Terminology needs to be adequately explained, especially if it is used differently in different disciplines, hence our use of a Glossary in this book to indicate how we are using certain words; statistical methods may need expanding on and acronyms always will; what counts as adequate discussion of your source material can also vary widely. For example, where simply noting the results or method of a previous study can be all that is needed in a chemistry paper, you would be expected to provide a greater degree of interpretation or evaluation in a history article.

Further, you may have to (re)consider the fundamental assumptions of different fields, in terms of values, forms of argument, or concepts of knowledge. Consider what counts as proof – or even a worthwhile topic to discuss – for an engineer, a philosopher, a physicist or a choreographer. Prepare yourself by becoming familiar with writing in the field you are venturing into, since you may need to justify aspects of your study that might otherwise be taken for granted; equally, your arguments may provide new ways for the field to advance. It may help to consider how different theories or thinkers have been influential in your field and beyond – often far removed from their original context of writing.

There are obvious cases where models or frameworks have been adopted by different fields, for example, Kuhn's notion of '**paradigm** shifts' spreading from scientific models to myriad elements of society and thinking; the taking up of Wittgenstein's ideas of 'language games' and 'family resemblance' in social science, theology, art criticism and in defining what constitutes a doctorate; or how a 'medical model' has influenced different forms of psychotherapy. Naturally you will not necessarily go into your cross-disciplinary writing with such game-changing ambitions, but it is interesting to note how different disciplines can re-purpose one set of ideas for their own needs. Having collaborators with different experience and outlooks will help with bridging these epistemological, technical or stylistic gaps; be prepared to challenge yourself and others, and this approach will reap significant rewards. Furthermore, building a good, frank relationship with your collaborator/s allows you to share and challenge ideas and perspectives before going 'live' to your wider audience.

Ultimately, you need to find and understand the best angle from which to make your contribution valuable – the big 'so what?' that all research needs to answer. Think about how your collaboration allows you to do things differently; make it explicit that your work can have value for others – or what they are missing out on if they do not take your work into account. Again, selecting the appropriate key words and title is essential here. Think of this careful selection as an important part of extending and fortifying your niche; lay claim to your expertise by suggesting how it can be relevant to others.

One further advantage of writing across disciplines is that you can often re-purpose existing material to new contexts, maximising the effects of your research. Although every publication will need to contain new material, linking your expertise to a new perspective can allow you to renovate data or insights for a range of 'might reads'. It is, of course, not as easy as cut-and-paste – and sometimes even harder to (re)write than to start from scratch – but with the bulk of the research under your belt, this strategy can yield multiple publications rather than only one. It also has the potential to establish your expert niche more firmly, cementing an association between you and your central interests. Part of this diversity may stem from pursuing different publication formats, too, as we explore in the remainder of the chapter.

Books

So far, we have concentrated on journal publication, since this is fundamental to most disciplines. In Chapter 7 we will look in more detail at turning your thesis into a monograph, which is common practice in humanities subjects. There are also other approaches to publishing books, however. Continuing the idea of collaboration, writing book chapters is a reliable way of widening the net of readers. The most common types are essay collections on a specific theme, conference proceedings and introductory texts. Unlike journals, such collections are normally the result of invitations to contribute, so will depend on your networking abilities and conference contributions. While we will not go into the Machiavellian art of conference networking here, it pays to keep abreast of the conferences that may lead to publications, academics who are planning a collected edition, and current trends in publishing and education. You will find a range of ideas to stimulate this in our sister book: *Success in Research: Inspiring Collaboration and Engagement* (Reeves et al., 2020).

The standing of the edited collection is currently the subject of some debate. These are less common or useful in the sciences but generally well regarded in the humanities and social sciences. There are definite upsides, even beyond the satisfaction of appearing in a print hardback. The collection links your work with that of other contributors, who may be more established, and in a well-planned collection there will be valuable connections between entries. You may be asked to read other contributions and adjust your own to highlight points of corroboration or different perspectives on the same material. This adds value to each part of the edition and may direct readers to you who would otherwise have only read a single chapter or essay. You can also spend more time on your own research and less on laying out the importance of what you are doing, since the editor's foreword will do much of this work for you. Further, for some collections there will be opportunities to be more creative or distinctive than with a journal that has a narrow format for all entries.

There is considerable variation in the longevity of collected editions. Some make little impact and disappear after the initial publication; others can be important points of reference for many years, especially if one or two of the chapters become very influential. Occasionally, a collection can become a solid textbook covering the topic, which will place it on library and student bookshelves for a long period. This can be hard to predict, partly because collected editions are not often anonymously peer reviewed. The quality of the book sometimes only becomes clear some time after publication; chapters must earn their standing rather than hitting a more easily noted 'standard' by appearing in well-known journals. Of course, collected editions can be just as rigorously compiled as journals, and demand just as many checks and reworkings; editors and publishers with a strong reputation for this will increase the perceived quality of their collections.

One downside to such books is that currently they are not automatically available online and rarely to **open access**. (This is gradually changing, however.) You also need to choose your writing style carefully and may have to conform to the editor's preferences for some areas. As ever, consider your audience, too. You may be writing for a small cadre of informed experts or a general scholarly audience. Are you introducing fundamental materials – for undergraduates, say – or entering an already highly-refined discussion? This consideration should orient your style and vocabulary.

The former will need to be clear and minimally technical, and should explicitly signpost the material covered and its relevance. It can be first-rate practice for designing your own teaching and, if the book is selected for a course, will ensure a large readership. As well as providing a grounding in the fundamentals of the topic, think about the aspects that excited you when you first covered this subject – striking facts, stories or arguments – and share these with your new audience. Again, contributors to such volumes are usually contacted by the editors, so getting yourself known as an excellent communicator of your area of expertise through conferences, posters, blogs or public engagements, and so on, can be crucial to getting the opportunity to contribute in the first place. In the case of the contribution to a refined discussion, the **language register** will already be explicit, and the importance of the topic taken for granted for you to elaborate.

Conference proceedings recruit in similar ways; you need to be at the conference to be considered. However, these do tend to speak to an already relatively expert audience. Like the edited collection, the editor's preface may do much of the scene-setting for you, and more demanding exposition may be permitted.

Other platforms

Moving away from the more traditional outlets for academic writing, you may wish to consider where else you can have meaningful impact. There is growing acceptance that academics need to exploit diverse channels to communicate their work with the public, other institutions, government and business. The degree to which any of these apply to your research will of course vary, but with a little creative thinking you may find new platforms through which you can establish yourself.

Simplest and easiest may be keeping a blog of your experience as a researcher. While you may not write up your research here, you can talk about topical or important matters, convey some of your own personality through pictures and informal writing, and build connections with others who follow your blog or contribute to discussions. This will not replace peer-reviewed and prestigious publication, but you can use it to point people towards your other work, publicise events and causes that matter, and make it easier for people to find you online. Depending on how you balance the professional and personal aspects of the blog, you may still find publication possibilities arising from it. As the publishing market becomes more diverse, several smaller presses have begun to specialise in shorter, less formal kinds of academic book; blog material can be a good starting point for writing up punchy, timely and accessible essays.

You can also find something of a middle-ground by writing critical journalism that communicates your academic knowledge on pressing topics. *The Conversation*, for example, publishes short and non-technical pieces in which academics make their own research relevant to current events – in politics, technology, environmentalism or health. If you have something to say and can yoke your research to something that wider society is concerned about, this is a great route to finding new and interested readers. This requires restructuring your arguments to suit the non-expert, but it is not just a matter of simplification; this can be an opportunity to make new connections with your own core studies, rethinking your subject matter from outside your usual research paradigm. Voice of Experience 2.2 shows how looking for a new take on your existing work can open new pathways to publishing.

Voice of Experience 2.2

Communicating beyond academia

For a side project of my PhD, I got involved with a group, a writing collective, dedicated to communicating beyond academic disciplines. I ended up producing work based on my research but then reformulating it several times to suit different audiences (almost in the reverse of the normal pattern!). The poetry exhibition led to a pamphlet publication, for which I wrote the introduction, explaining the philosophy behind it for a literary audience. I then turned this into a longer, more academic essay for an arts journal, using the installation to illustrate some points that would require specific background knowledge. Finally, the path this sent me down helped me to refocus one part of my PhD project, so I found I had a different angle on my material; I adapted some material from my thesis into a much more speculative paper, to present at a specialist conference. At each of these stages, the opportunity appeared through what I'd experimented with before – making unexpected links in person or online, and effectively inviting myself to collaborate on articles or projects.

Researcher in English

Another route to publication and recognition that researchers are not always aware of is work for policy bodies. The need for expert analysis of the large and complex issues of society is constantly growing, and policy bodies are expected to underpin their findings with strong data and analysis. Researchers have a host of valuable skills while stepping off campus to work on immediate and actual challenges can be very fulfilling. Several funding bodies value policy work as an outcome of their support for PhD studentships, and offer development opportunities for their cohorts; these are typically three- or six-month placements with a relevant policy body, working on a number of projects that benefit from your professional knowledge.

Policy documents produced by such organisations can vary widely, depending on their remit and reporting structures. However, they are generally intended to be read by non-specialists within a sector, with accessible handling of information and concrete recommendations. Clarity and conciseness are key, as well as mastery of the key ideas within this area. Aside from being a useful education in non-academic but professional communication, policy involvement can broaden your readership and help you stake your claim as an expert on the topic.

All the considerations discussed here connect to how we understand the idea of **knowledge transfer**. Although it can often feel like one of those institutionally sanctioned catch-all terms (surely transferring knowledge is a university's main purpose), it can make considerable sense to think about why you are communicating your knowledge, and to whom. Knowledge transfer is usually defined as mutually beneficial collaborations between research, business, public sector institutions and wider society. It can take the form of skills building, consultancy, licensing, businesses launched based on research ideas, or public engagement and publication.

It is important, however, not to view knowledge transfer as a one-way process, with universities producing the knowledge to bestow on end-users. Instead, it is worth considering how you can share your work in ways that will encourage reciprocal benefits. Research thrives on investment, debate, new data and the testing of ideas in new arenas. In just the same way, your publication strategy can spark new opportunities and resources. The key is to have clear objectives, both short- and long-term, and deliberate on how each different public can best interact with what you are doing. Make yourself the best conduit for this knowledge, recognising how (re)thinking your writing can enrich your own understanding. This may be a good time to revisit your strategy created in Activity 1.4 and elaborate particularly on Box 2. Before turning to the next chapter, which focuses on the peer-review process and how you can best navigate it, we offer you some top tips for connecting with, and benefiting from, your diverse potential audience.

Top Tips 2.1

Attracting different audiences

1. Seek out variety in your publications. Cover more ground and resist submitting repeatedly, and only, to journals you know are likely to accept you.

2. Research before you submit. What sort of material does the journal publish and for whom? Work rejected for not meeting publisher's requirements, or aimed at the wrong audience, is wasted effort.
3. Be aware of your own assumptions and position. Will your readers share these or do you need to explain them?
4. Say what you have to say clearly and invitingly. A carefully composed title and opening sentence can make all the difference.
5. Make the 'why' or 'so what' foremost and central in any article, abstract or book proposal. Do not make your reader or editor hunt for the significance of what you are doing. Be specific and realistic about the scope and importance of the research.
6. Focus on the most important information, what is most relevant to that specific audience. Be a tough editor of your own work.
7. Establish your 'disciplinary niche' and write from there. Even if you are working in an interdisciplinary situation, writing from within a discipline strengthens your academic standing and does some of the work of elucidating the key terms you rely on or introduce.
8. Say yes to scary things. Every time you do, you create new opportunities. Build collaborations that complement your own expertise.
9. Work with your editors and reviewers. They may seem like distant Olympian gods or meddling pedants, but their advice can make your writing clearer and more accessible. They are intent on ensuring high-quality work and a successful publication. It is fine to disagree with comments, but make sure it is not your pride getting in the way.
10. Do not stand still. Academic publication is a slow and deliberate business; waiting for one project or article to be finished can limit your visibility. Ideally, as we suggested in Chapter 1, you will always have one thing being written, another in the publishing process and another in the planning stages.

Further reading

Becker, L. (2014) *Presenting Your Research: Conferences, Symposiums, Poster Presentations and Beyond.* London: SAGE.

Clughen, L. and Hardy C. (2012) *Writing in the Disciplines: Building Supportive Cultures for Student Writing in UK Higher Education.* Bingley, UK: Emerald.

Reeves, J., Starbuck, S. and Yeung, A. (2020) *Success in Research: Inspiring Collaboration and Engagement.* London: SAGE.

Web resources

www.researchtoaction.org/wp-content/uploads/2014/10/PBWeekLauraFCfinal.pdf
www.cam.ac.uk/research/news/what-is-knowledge-transfer

www.newyorker.com/books/page-turner/why-is-academic-writing-so-academic

www.birmingham.ac.uk/schools/historycultures/research/news/2017/writing-and-editing.aspx

https://blogs.lse.ac.uk/impactofsocialsciences/2013/07/23/in-defence-of-edited-collections/

www.nytimes.com/2014/02/09/education/edlife/creativity-becomes-an-academic-discipline.html

https://23things2019.wordpress.com/

http://theconversation.com/uk

3

How can you make the peer review process work for you?

In this chapter you will discover:

- What peer review is and why you should engage with it
- Different types of peer review for a range of purposes
- How it works for conference papers
- How it works for journal articles
- How it works for books
- Preparing in advance for peer review
- How to deal with rejection
- The benefits of becoming a peer reviewer

What is peer review and why should you proactively engage with it?

It is not unusual for academic writers to view peer review with some trepidation. It is recognised that publication is essential to disseminate research and thereby build an academic reputation that could lead to secure roles and even promotion. It is also common knowledge that peer review is a hurdle to surmount in order to be successful in publishing academic work. In this chapter we explain the peer review process to prepare new authors for what to expect, drawing on the literature and on the experience of authors, editors and reviewers. By doing this, we aim to build the confidence of new authors to present their research to a critical audience. We also address some new and interesting developments in peer review, which may be the beginnings of significant changes to come.

Confidence increases with successful publication; however, successful publication often depends on the confidence with which the process of publication is embarked upon. Thus, our aim in this chapter is to provide information and guidance about peer review that will help you, whether as a newer researcher or a more experienced one, to understand the process and, on the basis of that understanding, to design a strategic publication plan with some degree of confidence.

Definition and purpose of peer review

Let us deal first with who the peers are. They are people like you. They are perhaps, but not necessarily, more experienced than you in writing/research, but they certainly are fellow researchers and writers within your scientific, academic or professional field who must also subject their work to peer review processes. However, that does not imply that they will be entirely sympathetic to your publication potential because they have an important role to fulfil: to evaluate submitted work to ensure that what is published is of good quality, meets standards of validity and adheres to the editorial standards set by the conference, journal or publisher that they represent. Frequently, they also have a duty to use their expertise to provide submitting authors with advice on how to improve their submission if they think it has some merit or, if they reject it, to provide cogent reasons that should provide guidance for future submissions. Thus, these reviews combine **formative** as well as **summative assessment** (see also our sister book, *Success in Research: Delivering Inspirational Doctoral Assessment* (Denicolo et al., 2020)).

The purpose of the process is to ensure that what is published is not only valid but relevant, with interpretations, based on acceptable evidence, that contribute to the debate in the field rather than simply being personal views. It is expected that such review will be both informed and rigorous so that the field is not contaminated by flawed or false results, nor is its reputation sullied by unscientific, unethical work or imprecise, poorly articulated communication. Further, review by peers is intended to indicate that published work is not only reputable and credible, but also relatively independent – free from any bias that might come from people with an economic or political incentive.

Advantages and disadvantages of peer review

Peer review acts as a useful filter for editors or conference organisers who receive more submissions than they can deal with. It helps them to identify the more important submissions from the more mundane and enables them to eliminate inadvertent errors and to suggest means of improvement to those submissions with potential for publication. Peer review also helps motivate authors to present their work more cogently, potentially driving up the quality of scientific publication.

However, while the process is accepted across academe, it is perceived to have some disadvantages, one of which is the time-consuming nature of the process and the delays this can cause to dissemination. There are also criticisms that it favours incremental research and knowledge-building, stifling innovation and protecting received wisdom. Another issue relates to the supposed anonymising of the peer review process. Often journals and to some extent publishing houses (see the differences discussed later between peer review of journal articles and books) include procedures intended to anonymise the process, either single-blinded (the authors do not know the peer reviewers, but the peer reviewers know the authors) or double-blinded (neither peer reviewers nor authors are identified to the other party). Despite this, many specialist fields are small enough and so well networked nowadays that 'informed guesswork' about either reviewers or authors can be quite accurate. We tend to know what colleagues are working on, what grants they have received for which research purposes, which results they have proudly announced at conferences and so on, and they know the same about us. Editors, too, have a role in the filtering and selection process, so human nature, with its strengths and weaknesses, can also play a part.

The value of engaging proactively

Despite those caveats, peer review is the process that currently determines what is published, so it is important to get to know the idiosyncrasies in the system and work with them. Until viable alternatives emerge, and you may contribute to that happy state (see the final section), you can save time, energy and ego by playing to both its strengths and yours and by avoiding the pitfalls that the uninitiated have frequently fallen foul of.

Certainly, the worst of those pitfalls is not submitting your work for publication for fear of rejection. This is the point where we can reassure you that all those famous authors whose work you value have, in their time, had some of their written works rejected. Similarly, most of your colleagues will also know that pain, and some, like your authors, will see it as par for the course. Those who successfully publish will know that each rejection provides a learning experience, an opportunity to hone their work to a greater quality and thus improve their 'hit rate'. However, it is important to push the potential of your publications by trying to get them into the most prestigious journals possible. Doing this will inevitably lead to more rejections than a strategy of submitting to journals that are not niche and attract fewer submissions and smaller audiences (see Chapters 1 and 2).

We cannot assure you that your skin will toughen; instead, we can help you to deal effectively with rejections and then put them aside to work on another offering with a greater understanding of the system. We can also draw on advice from experienced colleagues about how to reduce the possibility of rejection.

In our book on gaining funding for research, *Success in Research: Navigating Research Funding with Confidence* (Spencely et al., 2020), we advocate working with colleagues to gain feedback on draft proposals so that you can hone them to reduce rejection of grant proposals. Doing something similar with your academic writing is an informal way of gaining formative assessment from the very kind of people who will review your article or book proposals. Furthermore, from the experience of producing this book series, we can firmly assure you that none of the books would have come into being without our being able to get feedback and advice throughout the writing process from our colleagues and each other. Although we are not always kind, we try to be tactful because we recognise that it is far better for us to point out errors, non sequiturs, poor syntax or spelling errors than for them to stimulate rejection of the manuscript. We have also benefited from the ideas and perspectives colleagues have shared which helped us to improve on work that would eventually be submitted for external peer review of some kind.

Before delving into the formalities of external peer review, start your preparation by reading Voice of Experience 3.1 and then engaging with Activity 3.1.

Voice of Experience 3.1

The follies of inexperience

Reflecting on my first ever submission to a journal, I can't believe that I was so naïve. First, I made a fundamental error. I was so flattered by my supervisor suggesting that I should write a paper based on my **literature review** that I thought I would surprise her by getting it done and published quickly. Hmmm! It came back, fortunately rejected out of hand: fortunate because I hadn't realised that there was a protocol about ensuring that your supervisor should approve a submission. Fortunate too in that, on confessing my sins, my supervisor helped me to co-author a paper that was accepted by a professional journal.

Next, I was on my own as a new academic, drafting a paper in the expectation that I now knew what I was doing. I did think about running it by a couple of colleagues but felt shy asking for their time and, to be honest, was embarrassed in case they looked down on my efforts. Another lesson learnt, it came back with dozens of tiny typos noted and suggestions about elaborating on some points. The latter were useful; the former even more embarrassing than asking my colleagues to proofread. I'll know better next time.

A new academic

Activity 3.1

Identifying and recruiting informal and formal peer reviewers

There may well be colleagues in your department or school who review for journals, book publishers and the conference organisers for academic/professional associations and organisations. It would be well worth seeking their advice based on their knowledge of publishing interests and procedures. An email sent to the department stating your research and publication interests, seeking the advice of those with common or adjacent interests in exchange for refreshments, could start the ball rolling.

For colleagues with whom you work, you could suggest that you would be happy to proofread their writing as a reciprocal arrangement. If you know them well, they might be prepared also to share their draft and revised versions of prior publications, even their peer reviewers' comments.

Different kinds of peer review for a range of purposes

The general peer review process for journals

Peer review follows a relatively standard procedure with nuances or specific peculiarities added, depending on the specific publication type or editorial requirements. We strongly recommend that you refer carefully to editors' guidelines before putting fingers to keyboard. It is likely that they will make the important first decision about whether any submission is worthy of being forwarded to their busy team of reviewers. Such homework, including scrutiny of recently published work for topic interest and style conventions, can save wasted effort later.

The initial review stage, often called the 'desk evaluation stage', involves the chief or specialist editor checking the material for fit to their espoused theme or focus, and for fundamental errors or multiple errors, then rejecting immediately those that do not meet their standards. They may or may not inform authors of their reason for rejection. It is worth bearing in mind that some journals, particularly those with high-impact factor ratings, receive several hundred submissions in a month (and more in the run up to national research assessment/effectiveness exercises), a large proportion (up to 60%) of which are rejected at this stage.

Impact factors are determined by a calculation of citation indices so that the higher the citation rate, the more highly-ranked the journal and the greater the rejection rate (see Chapter 5). Thus, assiduous preparation is key, as is careful selection of your target journal after weighing the balance of likelihood of publication and prestige of the journal. (Thus, not every excellent article is published in a highly-ranked journal – authors have priorities and selection criteria too! There is also a global push not to overemphasise a journal's impact when considering the quality of research: https://sfdora.org/.) However, do avoid sending mediocre articles to **predatory journals** simply to raise your publication rate because it will undermine your professional reputation and that of your discipline (see Voice of Experience 3.2 and Information Box 3.1). We discuss journal choice in greater depth in Chapter 5.

Voice of Experience 3.2

Recognising predatory journals

I was flattered and amazed to receive an invitation to publish my research from a journal whose name I thought I recognised from the field, and so I began planning the article I would write for them. Serendipitously, I attended a meeting which involved a colleague who I knew was a reviewer for that journal. I told him how surprised I had been that the editor knew of my work. He was surprised too that I had been approached in that way, so I showed him the email. It was disappointing to find that it was not his journal, but one with a similar name. That was how I began my investigation into predatory journals, those that take fees for publications but do not have the standing of regular journals and do not provide legitimate editorial or publishing services.

I found out that having a similar name to a famous journal was a common factor, as was only notifying authors about fees after papers have been accepted, having fake names on editorial boards, having little quality control (reviews), non-existent impact factors and an aggressive approach to academics to submit articles or to join editorial boards.

I will be more suspicious in future of invitations that seem too good to be true.

Information Box 3.1

Identifying predatory journals

You can find on the web lists of predatory journals. One which is regularly updated is: https://predatoryjournals.com/journals/.

As we write, an article in *Nature*, 15 January 2019, by David William Hedding despairs of the South African practice of financially rewarding institutions and individuals for the number of articles published regardless of quality because it leads to the increased use of predatory journals and thus 'corrodes the quality of scholarship'.

Once your manuscript has succeeded in passing through the first filter of a reputable journal, it will then be sent for peer review, which is often a **'blind' peer review**. As mentioned earlier, **single-blind** refers to the author not knowing the identity of the reviewer, while **double-blind** reviews involve the identity of the author being obscured from the reviewer to reduce bias. There is now an alternative to the two blind review options: **open peer review**, which is explained in Information Box 3.2. Although open review is a less common form of peer review, with the whole Open Research agenda (see Chapter 9), it has been increasingly explored.

Information Box 3.2

Understanding open peer review

Open peer review comes in three main forms: (1) 'Open' meaning the use of 'non-blind' reviews. This means that both the identity of the author(s) and the reviewer(s) are known to each other; (2) 'Open' meaning that reviewer comments are published along with their name and affiliation so that the readership will see the reviewer's comments alongside the paper; and (3) 'Open' meaning that open access publication is accompanied by openly visible peer and/or public commentary, with or without formal peer review. If formal peer review is applied, this is also openly available alongside the publication and the open commentary.

The last of these options is certainly an antithesis of the traditional peer review processes, for which secrecy is paramount. The traditional model holds that anonymity ensures fairness and honesty. In contrast, these open models hold that transparency is a better answer to ensuring the integrity of the peer review process. This is an interesting and currently evolving debate that will be important for researchers to understand and to engage with. Leading the way in open peer review publishing is Wellcome Open Research, which has fully embraced the third form of open peer reviewing mentioned above: all versions of their publications are accompanied by peer review comments and open commentary with the aim of encouraging transparent scientific debate (https://wellcomeopenresearch.org/). It will indeed be interesting to see the results of such models as they are sure to influence the nature of peer review moving forward.

Whichever the specific review process used, peer reviewers are selected based on their expert knowledge; sometimes reviewers may be asked to attend to specific aspects, for instance, the relevance of the theoretical basis, the appropriateness of the methodology or the originality of the findings. The number of experts chosen depends on editorial policy. Their task is to recommend acceptance of the work as it is (rare); suggest small or large refinements, corrections or other amendments (between 10% and 20% on average); or suggest rejection. Once the reviews are all received, which can take about two or three months, as we warned earlier, the editor compares responses and comes to a decision, summarising the main points made and making the final decision that is conveyed to the author.

If the author decides to attend to the re-submission requests made, it is usual that the revised work is sent through the review process again, normally to the same reviewers until a consensus (accept or reject) is achieved. This can take a considerable time, sometimes a year or two beyond first submission. Although more than a two-year wait is exceptional, it can add to the devastation felt if the final outcome is rejection, so you might heed good advice to ensure that you have several papers going through the process simultaneously (see Chapters 1 and 2). You cannot submit the same paper to different journals, but the articles can be based on the same piece of research but with a different main storyline, analysis and/or emphasis, depending on the discipline and the specific journal's submission agreement.

It is worth making sure before first submission, therefore, that your article is well-thought through and carefully prepared. One means of doing so is to present your work first at a conference of peers to gain feedback from a wider audience than your immediate colleagues and friends.

The peer review process for conference papers

Submitting an abstract for a conference requires similar homework to that advised for a journal to ensure that your effort reaches the best, most appropriate audience. Any conference of significance will also have a peer review process, which can be as complex as for a journal article: the conference organisers first examine abstracts for relevance to theme and originality. They then usually have a panel of reviewers who make suggestions about which papers might be considered and why, based on originality, relevance and quality of expression. If there are topic streams within the conference programme, there may well be a convenor of feedback for each stream who recommends to the conference organising committee those papers that show the best potential and how they might be ordered in the programme. Thus, it is important not only to write a captivating abstract, but one that is clear about the content and concerns to be found in the delivered paper.

Some conferences have a two-stage selection process, the reviewing team sifting the short abstracts, then requesting the preferred ones to submit a longer version for final selection. Not all reviewing teams provide feedback on rejected applications; however, many of them, particularly professional societies, provide valuable feedback for improvement on those they intend to include in the conference or later in conference proceedings.

The richest feedback, though, comes from conference participants who either ask pertinent questions in the session or discuss the presentation's pros and cons more informally during breaks. Another publishing advantage can accrue from a conference presentation: the possibility of your paper being chosen, again by peer reviewers, as a contribution in a post-conference book. Some disciplines have very prestigious conference papers that are published in conference proceedings with impact to rival high-level journal publication, as mentioned previously (see Chapter 1). These submissions often resemble the process described above for journal peer review.

Of course, large conferences usually also include publishers' stalls, which provide opportunities for talking to publishers about the kinds of book they prefer to receive proposals for and what constitutes an effective proposal. Making contact with them can lead to unexpected publishing opportunities, as illustrated in Voice of Experience 3.3.

Voice of Experience 3.3

Making links with publishers is easier than you think

I strolled by the publishers' stands at the conference, noting that one was displaying several books on a topic near to my heart. Leafing through them, I got chatting to the gentleman looking after the stand. He said his colleague had gone for coffee but was the expert to ask about books in that topic area. He offered to introduce us. Expecting a bit of a sales pitch, I passed by later, and the introduction was made. What a surprise: by the time we had finished chatting, I had agreed to send him an outline of a book that I would love to write on the topic since he had expressed an interest in my ideas about the approach I would take and my enthusiasm for the task. I thought that was the last I would hear, but I received a follow-up email a few weeks later with detailed guidelines for writing a proposal. I am now on my second book for that publisher.

A proud author

The peer review process for books

Of course, you will realise by now that it is sensible to check with a potential publisher what their interest areas are and what they require in a book proposal. You should read through Chapter 6 in this volume, particularly the section on peer review. This should indicate to you that the process, while usually quicker at the proposal stage than that for an article submitted to a journal, is equally robust and frequently includes a peer review of the manuscript once the book has been submitted as a draft so that your ideas are evaluated twice and feedback provided on both occasions about how to make your book both interesting and saleable.

Preparing in advance for peer review

Cover letters

When submitting an article or a book proposal, in order to succeed in the first stage of review, you should use a cover letter to help persuade the journal or commissioning editor that your work is worthy of sending out for peer review. Although it is sensible to be concise (recognising how many submissions editors receive), you also must ensure that your submission stands out from the crowd. The letter should be formal, preferably addressed personally to the relevant editor (more homework to be done in advance), and should include important details such as the title and name/s of author/s and a brief rationale for your study that demonstrates clearly and strongly its novel findings and relevance to the journal's or publisher's readership (make sure you look this up on the journal's website and use their words as much as possible).

It is important to make a distinct declaration that the manuscript will be original, not published elsewhere, and that there are no conflicts of interest. It can be helpful to indicate any previous publications you may have, any links between this work and previous work published in the journal and also to suggest potential peer reviewers (if not requested elsewhere in the submission process), obviously choosing people who are both familiar with your work and are respected in the field. See Information Box 3.3 for further advice on cover letters.

Information Box 3.3

Cover letter templates

You should always read the author instructions prior to drafting a cover letter for any journal. Most will have very specific requirements that you must include, and what your journal of choice requires is the most important. Beyond that, there are sources online that can provide templates of cover letters to help you draft one. Here are two links from different publishing houses. Note the differences in requirements and styles, but also the commonalities: www.springer.com/gp/authors-editors/authorandreviewertutorials/submitting-to-a-journal-and-peer-review/cover-letters/10285574

https://authorservices.taylorandfrancis.com/writing-a-cover-letter/.

What to expect after submission

How to deal with feedback

Even if the reviewers see great potential in your written work, they may well have some suggestions or requirements to be met before they deem it publishable. Much of this feedback will be useful because it will help clarify issues or better inform readers. Occasionally, suggestions will be made that demonstrate that the reviewers have not understood your point. In that case, it is important to explain your ideas more accessibly. You may disagree with what reviewers suggest. If this is the case, we suggest you take a step back and perhaps give yourself a few days to think about the feedback you have received. Perhaps you could indeed explain your point more clearly. Perhaps your argument was not as tight as you thought. Do you think it is worth improving or do you think the review is not of a high quality? Then you have a choice of either conforming, withdrawing your submission or making a case for your perspective.

If you wish to have your written piece considered further, then you must respond to the editor and, through the editor, to the reviewers. Obviously, politeness is of the essence, so thank them for their consideration and their helpful comments. If there are changes required that you are comfortable to undertake, list them with a description of how you have addressed them. If the change does not really improve the paper but does not actually make it worse, accommodate it anyway. If you think that a suggestion/requirement would be inappropriate, respond to the positive changes first and then respectfully make a cogent case why you have not incorporated the change that in your view would be detrimental. Always ask yourself whether making a fuss is worth it, and if it is, present your view in a measured way.

Sometimes, frustratingly, you may receive conflicting or contradictory reviews, for example, one reviewer praising your conciseness and the other requiring elaborations; one asking for more detail, the other suggesting you reduce the detail. In that situation, you could choose to take the advice that you prefer and say why, or you could ask the editor to clarify which option would be preferable for their journal. Even after making the changes as you think they are required, reviewers will be asked to judge again whether the work is publishable in that journal. However, if you have handled it well, then it is unlikely to be rejected unless the journal is oversubscribed for the foreseeable future with really excellent papers. Thus, it is worth responding promptly.

Coping with rejection

Receiving a letter of rejection is never a joyous occasion. Our advice is to put it away in a drawer and mutter away to yourself for a day or so. Then retrieve it and consider the points made, whether they are valid, or whether there are suggestions that could improve your future writing or research. Usually there is something positive to be gained, if only the learning experience that the specific journal is not the best place to which to submit your work. It may be time to look at other publication options or consider doing a bit more research to strengthen the work. In either case, this is not a loss, and it should make the eventual publication, which will come if you are persistent, stronger and more impactful. Hopefully, you will take our advice and have another paper awaiting review and yet another in preparation so that you can move on productively. One other thing you might consider to ameliorate your frustration is to take on a role as a peer reviewer yourself.

The benefits of becoming a peer reviewer

Why do reviewers review?

We suggest that you consider becoming a reviewer, not for revenge, but to pass on what you have learned in the process and to reciprocate the efforts made by colleagues. Taking on this role is the best way to get a sense of what is required of written work for specific purposes. By recognising others' verbosity, you can learn to make your own work concise; by recognising the ambiguity in sentences written by others, you realise the importance of punctuation in your own writing. Importantly, becoming a reviewer gives you access to work at the cutting-edge of your field, stimulating ideas. See Voice of Experience 3.4, which presents a peer reviewer's perspective.

Voice of Experience 3.4

The benefits of being a peer reviewer

I became a reviewer for one journal early in my career while attending a presentation at a conference by its publisher who was looking for 'new blood' to join the team. I was honoured to be considered, and I learnt a lot about the criteria for a 'good' paper by combining my own instinctive responses to submissions with those comments provided by fellow reviewers which were sent with the revised papers.

I now review regularly for three journals, so I do restrict my reviewing for each one to those articles that are very firmly central to my field so that I don't get too many. This way it works out to be about six a year, which I can fit in. I find it helpful because, while keeping me conversant with what is happening in my area, I also have become familiar with each journal's style and requirements for an article. That in turn means fewer re-writes for me when I submit articles. After I draft a new one, I then nit-pick through it and ask a colleague to do the same using criteria we would use as reviewers for journals.

An established reviewer

We have already mentioned talking to publishers at conferences and, if you are not as lucky as our 'Voice' above in being recruited at a presentation, we would also recommend seeking out journal editors and enquiring about the possibility of joining the review team. Do not be shy about this; editors are always looking to recruit people who are expert in their field and willing to contribute in this way. Colleagues who currently review can introduce you to editors, and you can also meet them by joining in professional society activities. Even if you are as yet a doctoral researcher, you could offer to help your supervisor/advisor/mentor with their reviewing duties (watch out for the rush, though!). We provide, in summary, some top tips for becoming a good reviewer which, on reflection, may also inform your writing for publication.

Top Tips 3.1

Being a good reviewer

1. When you receive a review request, respond promptly, even if it is to say that it is not within your area of expertise.
2. If it is within your interest/expertise realm, then consider how much available time you have within the next few weeks and decide whether you might have a conflict of interests (if you are writing a paper on a similar topic, for instance) before responding in the affirmative.
3. Reviewing does take time – only take on a specific review if you can give appropriate time to reading the submission and commenting on it in a helpful way. It will certainly take several hours, more if you find you must reject it. Check the editorial policy before starting the review, ensuring that you are clear about your remit as a reviewer for that journal.
4. No matter how tempting it is to tell others of interesting findings, or to moan about a tedious piece of writing in an article you are reviewing, maintain confidentiality. Professional integrity demands this.
5. Start by reading the conclusion to determine novelty and interest to the journal.
6. Read the paper carefully. Note different aspects (differently-coloured highlighters or page-marker sticky notes are useful), such as good features, unclear points, typos, where elaborations might be useful, and so on. The volume of each of these is useful in deciding whether it is worth considering 'return for resubmission'. This also helps to organise your comments under categories for feedback.
7. Prioritise the content and substance rather than the presentation for which you can suggest ready revision procedures, especially if the author is a non-native speaker.
8. Check diagrams, graphs and tables carefully to ensure that they do demonstrate what is claimed in the text. It is easy to skip over these, although a flaw in the presented data can seriously affect a paper's publishability.

(Continued)

9. When the paper is outstanding, make sure that your review clearly notes this excellence; the journal editor will be delighted to include such an addition to the literature.
10. Provide constructive feedback whatever your final decision about recommending publication. Authors should know what to address and how to prepare for a re-submission, or why they are being rejected and how to improve future submissions.

When providing a review, put yourself in the position of the author receiving the feedback and decision, and when authoring an article, consider the reviewers' perspectives. Such reciprocity will help you to plan and hone your writing. We provide more detail about developing a writing plan in the next chapter.

Further reading

Cobey, K.D., Lalu, M.M., Skidmore, B., Ahmadzai, N., Grudniewicz A. and Moher, D. (2018) What is a predatory journal? A scoping review. *F1000 Research*, 7(1001). doi: 10.12688/f1000research.15256.2

Denicolo, P.M., Duke, D.C. and Reeves, J.D. (2020) *Success in Research: Delivering Inspirational Doctoral Assessment*. London: SAGE.

Haffar, S., Bazerbachi, F. and Murad, M.H. (2019) Peer review bias: a critical review. *Mayo Clinic Proceedings*, 94(4): 670–676.

Johnson, A. and Fankhauser, S. (2018) Engaging in the publication process improves perceptions of scientific communication, critique, and career skills among graduate students. *Journal of Microbiology & Biology Education*, 19(1): 1–8.

Kelly, J., Sadeghieh, T. and Adeli, K. (2014) Peer review in scientific publications: benefits, critiques and a survival guide. *e-Journal of the International federation of Clinical Chemistry and Laboratory Medicine*, 25(3): 227–243.

Memon, A.R. (2018) Predatory journals spamming for publications: what should researchers do? *Science and Engineering Ethics*, 24: 1617–1639. https://doi.org/10.1007/s11948-017-9955-6

Paltridge, B. (2018) Looking inside the world of peer review: implications for graduate student writers. *Language Teaching*, https://doi.org/10.1017/S0261444818000150.

Polka, J.K., Kiley, R., Konforti, B., Stern, B. and Vale, R.D. (2018) Publish peer reviews. *Nature*, 560: 545–547.

Spencely, C., Acuna-Rivera, M. and Denicolo, P.M. (2020) *Success in Research: Navigating Research Funding with Confidence*. London: SAGE.

Teixeira da Silva, J.A. (2019) Challenges to open peer review. *Online Information Review*, 43(2): 197–200.

4

How can you best plan your writing?

In this chapter you will:

- Focus on one publication, identifying your key message, target audience and publication type/location
- Learn methods for breaking down and planning your publication project
- Explore how to extend this planning to a larger and/or collaborative publication project
- Learn methods for getting started and overcoming writer's block
- Think about strategies to keep writing momentum, even when time is a limited resource
- Consider how to plan a publication from beginning to final publication in a way that makes the process less stressful and more enjoyable

From strategy to publication plan

Starting with your big picture

In Chapter 1 you identified the messages you wanted to convey in your publications and the specific audiences to whom you wanted to communicate. In this chapter, you will break down this overarching strategy and start to make it a reality by focusing on one specific publication, in order to plan that out from start to finish.

For this one publication, what is the key message you wish to convey, and what is the audience that you want to reach with this message? This is your first most important task and Activity 4.1 will guide you through it.

Activity 4.1

Finding your thesis

Every piece of writing needs a thesis. We are not talking here about the large tome that is the centrepiece of the doctorate. Here, we are using the word 'thesis' in its original Greek sense, meaning 'an intellectual proposition'. Every piece of research writing needs a specific argument running through it.

Take the time to think about what your main argument for this piece of writing is by answering the following questions:

- What is the key argument I wish to convey?
- What is my audience likely to think of this intellectual proposition? (Will they be shocked? Is it what they will expect?)
- What part of this argument will my audience care about most? (Note: this may be different from what you care about most)

Once you have thought about this key message and your audience's perspective on the key message, write one sentence that encapsulates your argument and addresses your audience's views on the topic.

This sentence is your thesis statement and should serve as your anchor for this publication. Post it above your computer while you are writing. Every part of this publication should be in support of this thesis. If you start to write something that is not, it should be cut (and perhaps saved for a different publication).

After completing Activity 4.1, you will know what your argument is and will have thought about how it relates to your specific audience for this publication. It is now worth contemplating the best format (chapter, article, book, blog, etc.), as well as the best location (journal, publishing house, platform) for the key message to reach this specific audience. In Chapter 1, we discussed these different choices in more detail.

By this stage it is likely that you have a fairly good idea where you would like this work to be published, whether that is in a specific journal or in a specific book, and so on. If you are not yet sure, it is worth doing some research, reading about the different options on their websites, discussing with a trusted colleague and, as suggested in Chapter 3, approaching potential editors or publishers with your proposed title (including your thesis statement) and learning whether this would fit well with their readership. Taking time to do this preparation can ultimately save considerable time as it increases the likelihood of acceptance of the final product.

Know what needs to be done

Once you have decided on where you would like to publish, ensure you have all the instructions and guidance for authors that are available. We would suggest pulling all this material together in a file, either virtual or physical, because you will be referring to it frequently throughout the writing and submission processes. It is extremely helpful to have fully read all the documentation before you start writing. Often there is guidance about style and language, as well as the format of the publication. There will be specific requirements for the presentation of references and figures, images and tables. All of this is easier to do if you know in advance and incorporate the requirements as you write. Thinking that you can simply put the entire publication into a specific format at the end is a mistake. In our experience, it is much more difficult to do this then, particularly as there are always several tasks involved in finalising a manuscript that take longer than expected (see final section). This means you can put yourself under much more pressure if you do not follow all the guidance from the start.

Guidance documents in hand, it is important now to think about your deadlines. These may be imposed by a publisher or editor, or by collaborators and co-authors, or may even be your own self-imposed deadline. Whatever the reason for the specific deadline set, we cannot stress enough the importance of having such a deadline. If you are making one for yourself, it will be quite important to do something to make this deadline real, so that the publication gets done. A very appropriate quotation here is: 'The easiest thing to do on earth is not write' by William Goldman. Without committed deadlines, it is likely you will end up 'not writing' quite frequently. Therefore, make deadlines and agree them with co-authors. If you are writing alone, tell your partner, your mother, or your mentor your deadlines so that someone will hold you to account, as well as be there to celebrate the end result.

Breaking down the task

You now have your thesis statement, you know your audience and where you are going to publish, and you understand the necessary instructions and have a final deadline. The next stage is to start planning the various aspects of the publication itself, which is important for several reasons. First, it helps you get started (which is discussed more in the next section). It also ensures that you stay on track and that you include all aspects that are important.

Outlining is a powerful tool to help break down publication tasks into sub-sections that can be more easily allotted specific time slots and deadlines. Outlining can be done linearly, creating what looks like an annotated table of contents. Alternatively, it can be done utilising mind-mapping techniques or even good old-fashioned post-it notes, which can be shuffled around to create the best flow order. Use the technique that works best for you. What is important is that you break down your argument into sub-sections and start to envision what the content of your publication will look like.

To begin outlining, start with your thesis statement and think about the key evidence and sub-arguments you wish to communicate to support this intellectual proposition. It may be that your publication already has a defined structure, which is common for journal articles (for example, introduction, methods, results, discussion). It may feel like this is already nicely broken down so that you do not have to think about outlining. However, from experience, what often happens in the absence of a good outline is that the author starts writing the introduction and methods, both of which end up too long and are often not directly related to the thesis statement. This can cause the results and the discussion section to feel dissociated from the first half of the publication, possibly leading reviewers to misunderstand the main points of the article. A good outline helps to ensure that all aspects of the publication work together.

If there is already a defined structure, we suggest that you use this structure and then within it define the key arguments and evidence you will present in each section to support the main thesis statement. If you have no pre-defined structure, as is common for chapters, books or other forms of publication, you will have to build the structure directly based on your outline. Once completed, you should be able to read through the outline and understand the flow of the publication, with the argument building throughout to make the conclusions at the end logical.

Once you have this structure, you can plan the specific times when you will write each section or sub-section. Many people instinctively start at the beginning, and this may well be the best course of action. However, with research publications, we find it is often best to start writing the research results first. This is the core of any research publication; it is the part that the readers will care about most. If there is a word limit, it is also the section that should take priority in terms of number of words. Starting by writing the research results also reduces the risk of long, rambling, introductory sections, and often works to sharpen the focus of a publication. Therefore, as you are planning what you are going to do and when, putting emphasis on the results or the most critical aspect of the publication is a good strategy. See Top Tips 4.1 for other planning tips.

Top Tips 4.1

Planning tips

- Plan ahead
    - Set goals
    - Allot enough time (this can be difficult for new tasks; allow more time for these)
    - Start early

- Plan in months, weeks, days
    - Stick to a disciplined schedule
    - Plan down to the hours if needed
    - Break tasks down into small chunks

- Prioritise tasks
    - Prioritise with your goals in mind
    - If you are having trouble getting started, complete quick tasks first
    - Keep your focus and avoid things that detract/distract
    - Strike a balance between tasks
    - Dedicate your best time to the most difficult tasks

- Give yourself time
    - Know your working pattern
    - Assign reasonable time lengths to tasks
    - Plan your down/relaxation time
    - Celebrate success along the way

- Reassess
    - Assess what has worked
    - Be honest about what has not worked and why
    - Adjust your plan to make it more realistic if necessary

Managing larger pieces of writing and collaborations

Managing larger pieces of writing, like a book or monograph, or coordinating a journal article or chapter with multiple collaborative partners, adds complexity to publication planning. Larger pieces of writing need to be well planned out from the beginning, with realistic time frames for each element. It may be tempting to work backwards from the deadline and allocate equal amounts of time to each chapter and consider planning completed. However, in our experience this is not likely to be the best way to realistically plan a lengthy writing project. First, chapters will take different lengths of time depending on the content. Some chapters will be written more quickly because you have previous material that you will be able to adapt and you know the subject well. Others may take longer, requiring more background reading or crafting of complex arguments. This should all be considered in the plan. Second, it is unlikely you will have the same amount of time to write each month throughout the course of a year. You will have very busy periods when writing at all may be a challenge, and you may have the odd week in which you are able to focus and produce thousands of words. This may be difficult to predict over the course of a long project, but it is worth considering as much as possible when planning. All this knowledge will help you set specific **milestones** with clear **deliverables**, so that you will know if your publication project is on track. See Information Box 4.1 to learn more about milestones and deliverables.

Information Box 4.1

Setting milestones and deliverables

Milestone: identifiable stage of completion

- Half-way point to the publication deadline

Deliverable: evidence of progress; a product

- a draft of a chapter
- a completed section

Why bother?

- When you have a big project with only ONE deadline at the outset, procrastination is a danger
- Interim goals help internal deadline-setting and scheduling
- When working with others, agreed milestones help everyone to see where progress is being made and what may be falling behind.

Deliverables should be SMART objectives:

- **S**pecific (what exactly are you going to do? For example, draft Chapter 4)
- **M**easurable (how will you know when you have done it? For example, chapter sent to lead author for feedback)
- **A**ttainable (is this achievable? For example, time planned into schedule, content of chapter defined)
- **R**elevant (is this goal helping me towards my publication aims?)
- **T**ime-bound (is there a realistic deadline?)

As discussed in Information Box 4.1, SMART deliverables, set to establish progress at specific milestones, are key to keeping a larger publication project on target. These become even more critical when working on a collaborative publication project. By ensuring that everyone involved in the authoring team has well-defined deliverables that are SMART enables you to identify everyone's individual contribution to the project. It is also extremely important to ensure that all collaborative authors are aware of each other's deliverables. This will highlight when one member's objectives are dependent on another's and identifies who a colleague can turn to if they have a question about another aspect of the project.

The agreed timeline for collaborative projects will have to accommodate the time constraints of all the authoring team in order to ensure delivery of the project. Fostering a collaborative spirit that supports open communication is also vital, so that authors can signal to the team if new challenges or obstacles in their life may cause deadline slippage, perhaps necessitating re-planning. As this authoring team can tell you, a year of adult life brings many ups and downs; working with colleagues who are supportive of each other in turn makes for not only successful projects, but enjoyable ones. Our sister book, *Success in Research: Inspiring Collaboration and Engagement* (Reeves et al., 2020), discusses collaborative authorship in more detail.

Getting started

Now it is time to start writing. As stated in Top Tips 4.1, it is helpful to plan your writing time for the periods when you are, or can be, the most productive. All of us have a time of day when our brain is most alert and creative; for some, this may be early morning, while for others, it may be in the evening once everyone else is in bed. This is an individual difference. What is common to us all is the fact that we do each have a time during which we are likely to be most productive. Use this 'best' time for your writing as much as possible.

Sitting at your desk (or wherever you like to write) at this optimum time of day and staring at a blank computer screen is likely to make you want to get a cup of tea or coffee, or perhaps check the news or a social media site. The look of a blank page is quite intimidating. Therefore, the best way to start is to fill this page quite quickly. You already have some material from the first part of this chapter, so we suggest you start by putting this down on the page. Type in your thesis statement and your outline. You may have other material that you want to include in this publication as well, such as figures or graphs or bits of writing you have already started. Slot all of this into the section of the outline in which you think it will probably end up. Then copy the section of your outline you are going to start working on right above where you will now start typing. This should give you a fair number of words on the page and will lessen the intimidating cleanness of the blank page, making it a little more inviting to add new words.

Dealing with writer's block

It is not uncommon for writer's block to occur at the beginning of a publication project, although it can occur at other times as well. If you find yourself looking at the computer and doing everything besides writing, you are not alone. This happens to all of us at some point. Luckily, there are a few techniques that can help get you writing so that you can keep your publication plan on track (also see Duke, 2018, in the Further Reading section at the end of the chapter).

The first important point is to remember that what you do in your daily writing sessions does not have to be masterful or eloquent; in fact, initially it is fine if the writing lacks clarity and structure. It is a common misconception among newer researchers that beautifully coherent prose and tightly constructed arguments just flow from the fingers of experienced academic authors. Believe us, we wish this were true but, alas, it is not. If there is a perfect word or phrase or argument, it is likely that it will take drafting and redrafting to find it.

Therefore, particularly in the early stages of a publication project, your main focus should be on putting words on a page, not ensuring that they are of quality. Through drafts, revisions, feedback and redrafts, those words can eventually be crafted into an articulate and honed publishable piece. At the initial writing stage, it is vital that you take steadily progressive steps towards your goals.

One technique that can help in freeing you from any writing block you may experience is **free writing**. If you have never used this technique, it is very simple to learn. You designate a specific amount of time, as little as two or three minutes, or as many as 20–30 minutes. What is important when you free write is that you write continuously, and you do not judge your work. It does not have to flow, it does not have to be grammatically correct, it does not even have to be in proper sentences. Your aim is to get as many words on to the page as you can. Writing is like a water tap, you cannot get to the hot water if you keep turning the tap on and off. You have to let the cold water flow to get to the hot. See Activity 4.2 for a more detailed explanation of free writing and for suggestions of different ways that free writing can be used to help you if your writing does not seem to be flowing.

Activity 4.2

Using free writing

Free writing is a versatile technique that can be used in many ways in various situations. Here we provide five examples of how free writing can be used to keep your publication project moving forward. Do, however, feel free to adapt these techniques to suit your own situation or to come up with other uses for free writing.

Exercise one: Becoming unstuck

If you are feeling stuck, sometimes starting to write directly about the topic at hand can feel too overwhelming. It may be helpful, first to do a short free-writing session about why you feel stuck. Write down the question: 'Why am I struggling to write?' or 'What am I finding difficult about writing this chapter/article/section?' Then set a timer for five minutes and start writing. During these five minutes, do not stop, do not judge, do not filter anything. Just let the thoughts come out. At the end, read what you have written and then perhaps do another similar free-writing exercise, either delving deeper into this question or moving on to Exercise two.

Exercise two: Clarifying your thoughts

If you feel you are at a stage where your thoughts are muddled, and you do not quite know what to write next, write down the question 'How does this section relate to my overall thesis?' or 'What is the main point I want to make in this next section of writing'. Set the timer for 10 minutes and free write. After 10 minutes, read what you have written, and then either give yourself another 5–10 minutes free writing to develop your thoughts or take a thread from what you have written and free write about this for 10 minutes. In the end you should have identified a line of argument you wish to pursue and have a considerable number of words that can now be crafted into the start of a coherent argument.

Exercise three: Using free writing to warm up for writing

It is always difficult to start writing at the beginning of a writing session. Starting a writing session by asking the question 'what will I write today?' and then free writing about the subject for five minutes is a good initial warm-up. It may be that you will then benefit from another 10-minute free-writing session focused on your identified writing objective for the day. Another useful strategy to keep momentum using this technique is to end a writing session by jotting down the topic you would like to write about during your next writing sessions. You can then use this topic as your writing warm-up. Whichever approach you use, this is a good way to get many words on the page quickly.

Exercise four: Developing your 'personal voice'

Particularly for newer researchers, it is common to receive feedback that your writing is not 'critical enough', or for more established researchers to become caught up in other authors' arguments and lose sight of their own view. Writing the question 'What do I think of _____ and why?' and free writing for 10 minutes can be a useful way of clarifying your

(Continued)

voice in your writing. By using free writing, you will be less likely to rely on references or to use other people's words, which can help you develop your authoritative voice and to better understand your own academic position.

Exercise five: Writing productively and efficiently

If you are short of time and balancing many different responsibilities on top of your writing commitments (as we all are at many points of our careers), free writing can help you write productively and efficiently. When you have a window of opportunity, even if it is just 10 minutes, set your timer and free write for that time. Make yourself write with no filter and just allow all your thoughts to flow. You will be surprised at how much writing you can produce even in relatively short periods of time.

All the above techniques can help you kick-start your writing and get you back on track when you feel blocked. We also suggest you utilise your research community. While free writing is powerful in enabling you to explore your own thoughts and to put words onto a page, discussing your thoughts and gaining insight from those around you can be even more inspiring. Have a coffee and chat with a colleague or share a very rough draft with a mentor. It can take courage to share work in progress with others, but the benefits are immeasurable. Furthermore, their experience and advice may save you considerable time and, as we all know, finding enough time is one of the greatest challenges to planning publications.

Finding the time

We have all done it: built the project timelines, put together the Gantt charts and to-do lists, created the best laid plans. Then reality collides with all your good intentions. Deadlines are missed and the guilt mounts, sapping the joy from the writing experience. While procrastination can be a problem, it is usually prioritisation that is the greater obstacle as important tasks tend to be overshadowed by those of a more urgent nature. Urgent tasks have immediate deadlines, such as the lecture you are delivering the following week, the data you are scheduled to collect, the meeting to prepare for the next day, or the emails that are filling your inbox awaiting an answer (whether those in fact are urgent is perhaps worth considering).

To stay on track with your publication plan, you must prioritise importance over urgency, at least for some part of the week/month. Time spent reading, thinking and writing is important work, and so you should set aside time for it. To help you to find the time, it is useful to reflect on all the work that you do each week and to decide what is truly important for your university, for your department and for your career. By relegating tasks that are not important in these three respects to a lower position on your priority list, you will have taken a necessary first step, even if it is difficult to do so, to free up time for tasks that will help you to stay on track with your publication plan.

The next step is to give yourself permission to prioritise your writing and your career, which can feel selfish. However, sharing your research and your academic insights with the world is far from selfish; it is of prime importance and is one way in which your research and its value to academia as well as to society will be made visible to others.

Prioritising writing is the next important step. This means creating space each week for writing. In our experience, the time that can be set aside for writing is never enough; nevertheless, having some consistent time that is dedicated to your writing and your academic thought is important not only for your own intellectual development, but also for your ability to make a difference in this world.

When setting aside time for writing, it is important to be pragmatic. The likelihood is that you will not be able to set aside considerable blocks of time during your busiest working weeks. However, even the busiest researcher can find time for writing, if only for just 15 minutes in a given day. Although 15 minutes per day is not sufficient writing time to see all your publication plans come to fruition, it can offer realistic, frequent, low-stress daily contact with your writing in your busiest times. This may be enough to keep moving your plans forward. See Reflection Point 4.1 to think about how you can best use the time you have available for writing.

Reflection Point 4.1

Time accounting

Reflect on your last typical work day. Using a high-level estimate, write down how you spent your time, indicating each task and the amount of time spent on it. Now define each task in terms of whether it was urgent or not (for the purpose of this task, define urgent as whether it could only have been done on this day). Next ask whether each task was important. (In this case, we define important as important for your career progression.) How much of your research time was dedicated to non-urgent, non-important tasks? What is the balance you have between urgent and important? Most project planning research shows that the key to quality lies in the ability to prioritise important but non-urgent tasks.

Time accounting, as exemplified in Reflection Point 4.1, can help you to identify those pockets of time that can be restructured and used for writing, if it is not already a part of your day. Restructuring this time requires some purposeful planning. Schulte (2015) uses a term called 'time confetti' to describe scraps of free time in our days that are filled with petty tasks. For the purposes of this chapter, we will use 'time confetti' not to describe petty tasks (though some may be), but as scraps of time you have to complete micro-tasks.

A useful strategy for accomplishing a large writing task is to write in a few small bursts. Indeed, many tasks of busy researchers are done in small bursts, for example, sending a follow-up email, ordering equipment, grading one paper, responding to an online survey. If you find yourself in an extremely busy period, you can use this strategy of writing in small bursts to be creative with when, and where, you write. Try keeping a notebook with you, either in digital or hardcopy form, so that you can jot ideas down as they come. Then, at the next writing slot you can find, even if it is just 15–30 minutes, use free writing to develop one of those ideas. See Activity 4.3 to find your time confetti.

Activity 4.3

Finding time confetti

If you do not have one already, create a schedule for your next working day. Look at some of the more substantial tasks on your schedule and see if you can break them into smaller pieces, tasks that take between five and 20 minutes of time.

Now consider your entire day's schedule, including, for example, commute, appointments, grocery store trip, and so on. Can you find some time confetti during your day? Do you have a train commute during which you can read a journal article? Do you have a 15-minute gap between meetings to free write some ideas? Can you find 15 minutes after a lecture to reply to student emails?

Lastly, if you do some of the work in pieces of time confetti throughout the week, can you create a more cohesive block for writing?

Some readers may not like the idea of filling their time confetti with micro-tasks instead of pauses for downtime. Some may need larger, uninterrupted pockets of time to work effectively. You must find a working pattern that suits your needs. The concept of time confetti is to identify those tasks that may take less time and to carefully consider when you can do them, and to then structure your day leaving unmolested stretches of time for the tasks that truly require space and time for thought, such as intensive writing, proofreading and editing.

If you find yourself going through these exercises and struggling to find any pockets of time confetti, our last piece of advice for this section is simply to make the time. Do not wait until you have the time: seize it. This may mean re-prioritising your workload and de-prioritising tasks that are urgent but not important to those that are important but do not currently appear as urgent. It may mean saying no to something else that might take your time. However, this time investment will pay off in the long run as investing in academic writing is important on many levels.

Creating and keeping the habit of writing

As you have worked through the sections of this chapter, you have hopefully thought about how much time you can carve out of a day/week to dedicate to writing. Ideally, your writing time should be scheduled during a time of day when you are most productive and creative. This may not be always possible, but you should aim for it and, at a minimum, ensure that some time is dedicated each week to writing. Make sure this time is in your diary so that others do not book things over the top of your dedicated time. To help you track this, you might wish to consider a website such as https://750words.com, which keeps track of your writing, gives you daily statistics on your writing and awards badges for your accomplishments.

When starting to build a new habit, it can be useful to remain mindful of the advantages of the habit. With writing, especially in the early stages when you may not have tangible outputs to show for the time spent, reminding yourself of the benefits of daily writing can help keep you motivated. Sword (2017) makes the point that an important advantage of daily writing is the opportunity to continually practise your craft. For newer researchers this is important because honing your work helps you to produce the quality of writing necessary for publication. For those of us with more experience, we need to keep practising our writing, just as an athlete needs to train before running a marathon. Thus, writing time can be viewed as your academic training and exercise programme.

Another benefit that will come from writing regularly is integrating your research practice, as well as your teaching and your evolving thoughts, into your writing about research. This may take time to develop, but by generating ideas through writing, your research will expand and be informed by your writing, and vice versa.

Once you have found a time and space that works best for your writing, you may want to start implementing other habit-building behaviour into your routine to help the habit stick. One of the popular pieces of advice for habit building is to commit yourself to others. Committing yourself publicly will help with motivation and accountability. You could join or create a writing group that helps to hold one another accountable to your writing tasks. You may want to consider online writing communities if you do not have close-by peers with whom to write. This also allows you to spend more time with people who model the habits you want to mirror if the group is successful. You could even make this part of your promotional strategy by writing a daily blog or sharing on Twitter (see Chapter 10). Your followers could become those to whom you are accountable for daily updates and pieces of writing.

Another useful technique for turning writing into a habit is to build a routine or ritual around your writing, such as making a cup of coffee or tea, or having a snack prior to your writing. Having a specific place that is only used for writing can also help: as soon as you sit there, you orient your thoughts to writing, which prepares you psychologically and physically for the task. Lastly, on the days you really struggle, remind yourself of the benefits and your own motivation behind the exercise, and promise yourself a reward.

Planning the end stages

It is important to consider not only the time it takes to create a first draft, but also the time required for redrafting, editing and proofreading your writing. Generally, editing refers to the process of making changes to the structural and conceptual elements of your writing. For example, when you edit your writing, you will look for problems relating to the logical ordering of paragraphs. Perhaps you discover that one paragraph does not link logically with the previous one, so you need to insert another or reorganise them to create a seamless, logical flow. When you insert that paragraph, or reorganise paragraphs, you are editing your work. Sometimes, you notice that what you have written could be understood in two ways, making it ambiguous. When you make changes to remove the ambiguity, you are editing, which contrasts with proofreading, where you look for the more superficial errors in your writing relating to grammar, punctuation, spelling, formatting, etc. Top Tips 4.2 provides further tips on how to edit your publication.

Top Tips 4.2

How to edit your journal manuscript

1. Never edit immediately after you finish writing. You need to switch your mind off from the paper before you edit it, so that you can be more objective about it. Go out for a coffee, go shopping, or meet up with a friend before you start to edit.

Ideally, wait 24 hours before editing. However, sometimes deadlines mean that you cannot wait that long. Then, take as long a break from the paper as you can before you begin the editing process.

2. In your first round of editing (and there should be more than one), focus on *whether you have generally achieved what you set out to achieve*. This is likely to be a short round.

3. If you are happy that you have achieved your aim, then do your second editing round, which might focus on *whether the arguments are clear and logical*. Do not look for anything else in this round; if you spot a proofreading error, do not be tempted to put it right (unless of course, that is the cause of the break in logic or clarity). Keep to the focus of the editing round.

4. In your third round, look for *repetition or ambiguity*. Remember, repetition can include repetition of ideas in paragraphs, words in sentences, or it might even be repetition of entire paragraphs if you have accidentally clicked on 'copy and paste' instead of 'cut and paste' during an earlier editing round!

5. After three editing rounds, you are probably ready to do the *final polishing and proofreading* of your manuscript.

Here is a useful checklist for the final read through of your publication:

- Is your writing style consistent throughout the paper or have you lapsed into an informal or very formal style in places?
- Does your Introduction include a paragraph outlining the structure of the paper?
- Do the aims of the paper in the Introduction match the claims made at the end of the paper?
- Is the paragraph flow clear and logical?
- Have you included in your manuscript any keywords that are listed under the abstract?
- If you would like to find out more about maximising your chances of getting your article published, why not click on this link from *The Guardian*, which has tips from editors on how to get published: *How to Get Published in an Academic Journal: Top Tips from Editors* (https://www.theguardian.com/education/2015/jan/03/how-to-get-published-in-an-academic-journal-top-tips-from-editors).

The amount of time it takes to edit, redraft, receive feedback and redraft again is often underestimated. It is important to consider this phase in your publication plans, particularly when working to fixed targets and deadlines. The stage immediately before submission is likely to take twice as much time as you may think if you are new to the publication process. We would recommend clearing some space within your diary for the two weeks in advance of your publication deadline to ensure you have time for the final tasks. Put this in as fixed appointments and do not let anything displace this time; you will probably need it.

The other aspect that tends to be underestimated is the amount of time it takes for final completion of the publication, post submission. There is likely to be a delay while the work is out for review, but at some time in the next few months, there will be comments that need to be responded to and changes to be made. Final proofs will need to be checked and all details will need to be confirmed with the publishers. Good planning must take all of this into consideration to ensure the project can be delivered to schedule. It is often a long and complex journey from idea to eventual publication; however, seeing your research and your ideas in print and available to inspire others is truly one of the joys of being a researcher.

In the next part of this book, we will help you better understand how to write specific types of publication, aimed at a range of different audiences. Then in the final part of the book, we will explore how you can ensure your publications are visible to the largest audience possible and produce the greatest possible benefit to the world.

Further reading

Becker, L. and Denicolo, P. (2012) *Success in Research: Publishing Journal Articles*. London: SAGE.

Day, T. (2018) *Success in Academic Writing*. London: Palgrave.

Duke, D.C. (2018) When the words just won't come. In K. Townsend and M.N.K. Saunders (eds), *How to Keep Your Research Project on Track: Insights from When Things Go Wrong*. Cheltenham: Edward Elgar.

Powell, P. (2015) *How to Get Published in an Academic Journal: Top Tips from Editors*, The Guardian. https://www.theguardian.com/education/2015/jan/03/how-to-get-published-in-an-academic-journal-top-tips-from-editors

Jensen, J. (2017) *Write No Matter What: Advice for Academics*. Chicago, IL: University of Chicago Press.

Reeves, J., Starbuck, S. and Yeung, A. (2020) *Success in Research: Inspiring Collaboration and Engagement*. London: SAGE.

Schulte, B. (2015) *Overwhelmed: Work, Love and Play When No One Has the Time*. London: Bloomsbury.

Sword, H. (2017) *Air & Light & Time & Space: How Successful Academics Write*. Cambridge, MA: Harvard University Press.

PART II
Writing in different genres

5

How can you write impactful journal articles?

Guest author: Kate Turner

In this chapter you will:

- Discover how to engage with journal ranking systems and Quartile One journals
- Examine the audience of Quartile One journals
- Explore the headline of your research and articulate its significance
- Examine techniques for authoritative, clear and concise writing
- Think about long-term strategies to develop your writing for impactful journals

Writing a paper for a **Quartile One journal** takes time and effort. Selection for peer review is competitive and the process itself can feel intimidating, but it is definitely not impossible. The present chapter demystifies the world of Quartile One or Four Star journals and provides practical writing advice on how best to present your research for the editors of these journals and their audiences. In this way, this chapter is for anyone who would like to publish in Quartile One journals and is prepared to put the work in, but who may also feel confused by the process and unsure of what editors are looking for in a paper. Reassuringly, we would posit that these are feelings shared by most researchers, including those lucky enough to have published in **top-tier journals**.

What are quartile one journals and how can you engage with them?

The seemingly interchangeable terms 'Quartile One' (Q1) and 'Four Star' (4*) provide the first stumbling block for the researcher new to this form of publication. Both terms refer to the rank of the journal; either from Quartile One down to Quartile Four or from Four Star down to One Star. Different ranking systems, or journal bibliometrics, use either the quartile or star system to measure the journal's 'impact score', essentially meaning that the more the research from the journal is cited, the better the score. Tools such as Scimago Journal & Country Rank (SJR), Altmetrics, JRank, CiteScore, Impact Factor, and Source Normalized Impact per Paper (SNIP) are helpful for gauging the impact of journals as well as the reach of your own research. Chapter 12 will provide further guidance on different forms of bibliometrics.

Scimago Journal & Country Rank (SJR) is particularly helpful for identifying the reputation and prestige of different journals so that you can work out to which ones you may wish to submit your paper. SJR allows you to filter by subject area, subject categories and country so that you can see the journals in a specific subject category ranked from Q1 through to Q4. You can then click on a specific journal to see the history of its citation rate and impact score. Activity 5.1 will get you thinking about the journals that could be right for you. In addition to applying your own filters, scan the top 50 Q1 journals in any subject area in the world. You will notice lots of 'big names' on the list; Q1 journals are highly regarded journals with wide audiences. Indeed, while technically Q1 and 4* refer to quantitative systems that measure impact, conversationally, academics use Q1 and 4* to refer to reputation. Activity 5.1 will help you identify journals that you might consider.

Activity 5.1

Identifying the Q1 journals relevant to your research

Using SJR, narrow the search criteria to your discipline, and look over the top 10 journals. Are there any specific ones that you have cited a lot in your own research? This might be a good indicator for the journal most appropriate for you.

Draw up a list of the top four Q1 journals you would like to submit your paper to. Prioritise the journals that are the most relevant for the topic of your paper.

So, what qualities do papers published in such highly-regarded journals have? The UK Research Excellence Framework (REF) provides terminology that is often used to encapsulate the 'star quality' of these journal articles. Indeed, the term 'four star' has entered academic language as a result of the REF, the first of which was completed in its current form in 2014. The REF ranks research outputs (not just journal articles) from different university departments from 4* to 1* based on their 'output', 'environment', and 'impact'. The REF defines 4* research as 'world leading', 3* research as 'internationally excellent', 2* research as 'recognised internationally', and 1* research as 'recognised nationally'.

The REF's term 'four star' research is not the same as a 'Four Star journal'; the REF ranks research while journals are ranked by the amount that the papers in them are cited. They are, however, related in that Q1 journals tend to publish papers that score well in the REF because they have high 'impact'. As such, it is common to hear the phrase that Q1 journals publish 'world leading' research. This means that the editors of Q1 journals are looking for papers that present rigorous, original results that will be of interest to a wide audience.

By the time you have navigated the confusing relationship between the various rankings, you might be feeling some level of **impostor syndrome**. Do not worry; it is confusing and is something that researchers may only work out if they are lucky enough to be in a very supportive department with openly-sharing mentors and senior colleagues. Even in such a team, many academics discover these things by stumbling through journal submissions and the REF process in the early part of their career, so you can assume you are not the only researcher who feels this way. The fact that this process seems strange and obscure at times does not mean that you cannot excel in it. It is also important to acknowledge that no academic has ever sat down at their desk to write a 'world leading' paper.

'World leading' is a nebulous and overwhelming term and, although it is a common definition of high-quality research, focusing on this term alone is likely to lead only to writer's block. It is important to tackle this feeling of impostor syndrome because the guidance on writing for Q1 papers in this chapter will be useless if you never get around to writing up the paper because the world of Q1 journals just seems too intimidating. Remember that if you are completing, or have completed, a PhD, then you already understand how to achieve novelty in rigorous research, and this next step is simply working out how to make your research as relevant and accessible to as many people as possible. It is important to remember that 1* to 4* research is currently taking place across doctoral, early career, and senior academic levels; the rankings reflect research, not the number of years of experience. If you have something new to say that is important to a wide audience, then this process is open to you.

Your job, then, is to tell the story of your research as clearly as possible. See Activity 5.2 for a guide to getting started with this.

Activity 5.2

Finding the excitement and significance in your research

If you were given a blank piece of paper on which you could write one sentence that is, for you, the most exciting and significant thing you have found in your research, what would it be?

Try writing it down now.

Next, take a moment to consider *why* your finding is exciting or important. If this was not included in your first statement, add another sentence articulating this. Doing this will help you to hold the originality and significance of your research clearly in your mind.

Then, imagine you are told that this message can be shared by researchers around the world. How would you phrase it? Make these edits to your sentence now. This prompts you to rephrase any words you think they might not understand or might need clarification and is one step towards making your research understood by a wide audience.

Take a look at what you have written. These two sentences could form the 'headline' for your research.

Communicate one conclusion to a wide audience

Now that you have made a start on crystallising in your mind the main conclusion from your research, let us consider the opening sentences of the abstracts from three articles published in Q1 papers, presented in Reflection Point 5.1, to examine any commonalities in their writing styles.

Reflection Point 5.1

Commonalties in published abstracts

Read the following introduction sentences from three Q1 papers spanning a range of disciplines. Think about the language they are using. What do they have in common?

1. 'Feminist scholars have long critiqued the fashion industry's ultra-thin beauty standards as harmful to women. Combining data from three qualitative studies of women's clothing retailers – of bras, plus-size clothing, and bridal wear – we shift the analytical focus away from glamorized media images toward the seemingly mundane realm of clothing size standards, examining how women encounter, understand, and navigate these standards in their daily lives.' (Bishop et al., 2018)
2. 'Mental health problems are inseparable from the environment. With virtual reality (VR), computer-generated interactive environments, individuals can repeatedly experience their problematic situations and be taught, via evidence-based psychological treatments, how to overcome difficulties. VR is moving out

of specialist laboratories. Our central aim was to describe the potential of VR in mental health, including a consideration of the first 20 years of applications.' (Freeman et al., 2017)

3. 'In this study, the thermal comfort of the occupants of learning spaces using three different ventilation strategies (i.e. air-conditioning [AC], hybrid [HB], and natural ventilations [NV]) was investigated at a tropical university campus. Data were collected from 1043 survey questionnaires; concurrently, on-site measurements in three consecutive years were analysed.' (Lau et al., 2019)

Note that, even on an initial glance, all three of these extracts are relatively easy to follow, which is quite a feat considering that they span the humanities, psychology and engineering. Importantly, unless you are an expert in women's beauty standards, VR and mental health, as well as ventilation strategies in tropical climates, your ability to read these articles is not related solely to your disciplinary knowledge of these areas. This is important because editors of Q1 journals are looking for articles that appeal to the entirety of their readership, not just to one subsection of it. Activity 5.3 will help you to think further about your audience.

Activity 5.3

Exploring the potential audience for your paper

Look up the top three ranked journals in your general area of study. Now think of the various people who could comprise the audience for that journal. It will, of course, include researchers like you, but it may also include the retired academic, the browsing undergraduate student, or the librarian ordering the journal for general interest. It will also include researchers in your general area of study but who have a very different specialism from you. The editors of this journal do not have only you and your colleagues in mind; they will seek articles that can be understood by all these people. This is why the headline of your research and why it matters should form a clear pathway throughout your paper. When reading papers like this, editors can imagine their whole readership engaging with the paper and will be more likely to pass it on for peer review.

So, what makes the opening sentences in Reflection Point 5.1 so easy to follow for such a wide audience? Primarily, they focus on communicating just one key idea. For all three of these articles, you could imagine someone recommending it to a colleague, saying, for example 'it's about the uses of virtual reality in mental health'. Return to the headline you wrote for your own research in Activity 5.2. Could you imagine someone saying 'it's the paper about …' in just a few words?

If not, take the time to simplify the statement even more. You may find yourself thinking 'but if I simplify it, then I am watering down my study'. Most researchers, particularly in the sciences, are trained to write up their methods so that another researcher can replicate their study. This is certainly good advice. However, the people who might replicate your study are only a fraction of the audience for a Q1 journal. Unfortunately, if the editors think you are only catering for these people, then they might recommend your paper is published in a more specific journal.

You need to strike the balance and cater both for fellow researchers in your specialised field of study and for the academic in your more general field who has a subscription to the journal and wants to browse all the articles in it. Your specialist reader should be able to replicate your methods section, but your general reader should also be able to follow it sufficiently to understand how it connects to the headline of your study. It is like teaching a class composed of final-year master's students and first-year undergraduates: you need to be clear enough on the technicalities but also emphasise the importance, significance and excitement of the study. We are not suggesting that this is an easy process, but it is made far more difficult if you try to take a very specialised write-up of your work and edit it down or 'simplify' it. You will have more success if you start with the one clear headline and build the rest of the paper around that.

You may also struggle to simplify the headline of your research because you are trying to include two or more key conclusions. If this is the case, it is important that you take the time at this stage to isolate one clear conclusion for your journal paper. Papers that contain multiple conclusions might be written very clearly, but can you imagine yourself saying to a colleague 'it's the paper about A ... and about B ... and it finally suggests C'? If you find that your headline is looking a little like this, you may need to cut some of this away. It may be that you actually have two stories to tell about your research as two different articles. It may also be that you are still writing your way into the project in order to clarify what it is about. This is perfectly normal in most writing projects, but once you have crystallised your one key conclusion, you need to start the paper again, focusing only on this one idea.

Additionally, while each of our example articles communicates one key conclusion, the significance of that conclusion is just as obvious. In our three examples, for instance, we could very quickly say: 'women feel less stigma about their bodies', 'virtual reality might help people with mental health conditions', and 'researchers at a tropical university campus can work at a comfortable temperature'.

The obvious significance of the research is important because this is what makes people click on the article, want to read further, or talk about the research with others. Editors are interested in this. Note that none of our extracts actually uses words like 'novel', 'new' or 'significant'; the significance of the research is self-evident. This comes from the researchers being absolutely clear on why the research matters from the very beginning of the article. Engage with Reflection Point 5.2 to think about the significance of your research in more detail.

Reflection Point 5.2

Why does your research matter?

Now that you have thought about the headline for your research, take a moment to pause and consider why it matters. This might be very obvious to you, but will it be obvious to somebody outside your field? It can be helpful to clarify in your mind what kind of importance your research has. It is common for research to be significant for one of the following four reasons:

- It provides firsts in the field (for example, DNA, Dolly the sheep, the hadron collider)
- It proposes new methods (for example, new technologies for reading brainwaves in children)
- It is important economically (for example, we can make solar panels more cheaply)
- It has social benefit (for example, an improved policy for the protection of LGBT+ people)

What kind of significance does your research hold? This can help you to embed the importance of your research into your headline.

You may find that two of these are linked. For example, because you used a new method you might have proven a first in the field. This does not mean you need to exclude one of these from the article, but you do need to decide which one you will emphasise.

Writing authoritatively

Once you are clear on what you want your audience to know and why, you can focus on the technicalities of your writing to help convey those ideas. Writing in Q1 journals is authoritative, clear and concise.

Authoritative writing is borne to some extent from the pre-writing activities you have already completed; being clear on exactly what you want to communicate helps you to command the narrative. Having thorough control over your narrative also indicates authority; not only do you know the topic, but you are also able to guide the reader through it. Being decisive about your use of active and passive voice is one of the most prominent areas where you can take control of your writing. Consider the examples in Activity 5.4.

Activity 5.4

Comparing the active and passive voice

Two of our examples from Q1 journals are written in the active voice. Compare how they sound when converted to the passive voice:

Example 1

Active: 'Feminist scholars have long critiqued the fashion industry's ultra-thin beauty standards as harmful to women.'

Passive: 'The fashion industry's ultra-thin beauty standards have long been critiqued by feminist scholars as harmful to women.'

Example 2

Active: 'With virtual reality (VR), computer-generated interactive environments, **individuals can repeatedly experience their problematic situations** and be taught, via evidence-based psychological treatments, how to overcome difficulties.'

Passive: 'With virtual reality (VR), computer-generated interactive environments, **problematic situations can be repeatedly experienced by individuals**. They can then be taught, via evidence-based psychological treatments, how to overcome difficulties.'

In the first example, the clarity of the sentence is reduced when it is converted into the passive voice; the reader does not know why they are reading about 'the fashion industry's ultra-thin beauty standards' until they reach the end of the sentence, which provides the information that this is a critique by feminist scholars. Use of the active voice not only makes the sentence more concise, but the reader understands more quickly the point that the author wants to communicate.

In the second example, use of the passive voice places the emphasis on the 'problematic situations' rather than the individuals who can experience them using VR. In this way, the passive voice can shift the emphasis away from the important part of your sentence. The clarity of this sentence is also reduced by the passive voice as we need to start a new sentence in order to contain the final piece of information. In contrast, in the active voice, the authors are able clearly to express that the individuals do two things: 'experience problematic situations' and 'overcome difficulties'.

Academics often write in the passive voice as a hangover from the instruction to undergraduates not to use 'I'. Writing for journals requires more active decision-making around the active and passive voice. Note that examples one and two comfortably use 'we' and 'our' to express what they did in the research. The third example, however, is constructed using the passive voice:

> In this study, the thermal comfort of the occupants of learning spaces using three different ventilation strategies (i.e. air-conditioning [AC], hybrid [HB], and natural ventilations [NV]) was investigated at a tropical university campus. (Lau et al., 2019)

The use of passive voice here emphasises the investigation of the ventilation strategies rather than the researchers who did the investigating. Importantly, the researchers have chosen this writing style because they are clear about the most important part of the sentence. So, using the passive voice for the sake of simply avoiding using 'I' or to make the writing 'sound complex' does not help you write authoritatively. If you do use the passive voice, make sure that you are consciously choosing to use it to draw the reader to what was done rather than who did it because that is the most important aspect of the sentence for the reader to understand. In this way you are still the authority controlling the narrative.

This discussion of active and passive voice highlights a common misunderstanding in academic writing: you cannot use the writing to 'gloss' your ideas. This is because good writing is meant to disappear and let the ideas stand for themselves. For this reason, it is not possible to write up two-star research as if it is four-star research. However, it is definitely possible to write up four-star research as if it is two- or three-star research. In the next sections, we work on helping you develop techniques to make sure that you write your research to the standard it deserves.

Techniques for clear and concise writing

Clear and concise writing really does come down to the level of your words and sentences. Often researchers reach a point where they consider it somewhat 'high school' to think at this level. However, it is often attention to the detail of these technical aspects of your writing that can improve the clarity and precision of your expression and highlight the importance of your research. In Example 5.1, we have changed some key words and word order in the opening paragraph of a Q1 article to illustrate some common errors.

Example 5.1

Careful wording for clarity

Original version

Title: Democracy and Financial Crisis

'Over the past several centuries, **financial crises** have been frequent, widespread, and consequential. Charles Kindleberger counts over fifty international **financial crises** and panics since the seventeenth century. **More recently**, Reinhart and Rogoff have identified about 700 country-years of **banking crises** since 1800. **Financial crises are associated with adverse macroeconomic performance, most notoriously the depressions of the late nineteenth and early twentieth centuries and Japan's lost decade of the 1990s.** The US subprime crisis and the Euro crisis have underscored the salience of **financial crises** in the current era and also revealed important gaps in political science scholarship on the issue.' (Lipscy, 2018)

Edited version

'Over the past several centuries, **financial crises** have been frequent, widespread, and consequential. Charles Kindleberger counts over fifty international **economic emergencies** and panics since the seventeenth century. More recently, Reinhart and Rogoff have identified about 700 country-years of **banking crunches** since 1800. **Adverse macroeconomic performance, most notoriously the depressions of the late nineteenth and early twentieth centuries and Japan's lost decade of the 1990s, are associated with fiscal predicaments**. The US subprime crisis and the Euro crisis have underscored the salience of **monetary crises** in the current era and also revealed important gaps in political science scholarship on the issue.'

First, note what happens to the clarity when we substitute the recurring phrase 'financial crises' with other terms such as 'economic emergencies', 'fiscal predicaments' and 'monetary crises'. While all of these phrases mean roughly the same, there are important differences between them, and by the time we have read a few variations of the same phrase, the meaning is much vaguer. It is common when editing work to try to eliminate reoccurring words so that our writing does not sound repetitive. However, there is a balance to strike here; in this article 'financial crises' are the key words of both the title and the article, so it is important to return to them wherever relevant. This helps guide the reader through the article and so adds to the authority of your writing. Strong and consistent key words also make the one main headline of the article very clear throughout the writing.

Second, the emboldened sentence shows the reordering of words so that more complex information is placed at the beginning rather than the end of the sentence, making the sentence more confusing. Communicating complex information clearly is a hallmark of all good academic writing, but it is absolutely essential when preparing your work for a Q1 journal. The original sentence uses a helpful process in that it starts with the simplest piece of information, 'Financial crises are associated', then moves to the more complex 'adverse macroeconomic performance', and ends with the most complex 'most notoriously the depressions of the late nineteenth and early twentieth centuries and Japan's lost decade of the 1990s'. This formula means that the reader does not have to hold the most complex information in their head while taking in the information from the rest of the sentence. Additionally, once the reader has reached the most complex information, they have enough context to understand why they are being told this information. This is a helpful, stepped process to break down and simplify complex information that you need to communicate in your paper.

The next illustration, in Example 5.2, is taken from another Q1 paper and furthers our engagement with sentence structure.

Example 5.2

Simple versus complex sentences

Original version

'Excessive alcohol use is a leading contributor to morbidity and mortality. One in 20 deaths worldwide is attributable to alcohol consumption, as is 5.1% of the global burden of disease.' (Walters et al., 2018)

Edited version

'Excessive alcohol use is a leading contributor to morbidity and mortality, **indeed**, one in 20 deaths worldwide is attributable to alcohol consumption, as is 5.1% of the global burden of disease. **Alcohol used in excess is a global issue and if curbed could reduce death rates worldwide**.'

In this example, we increased the complexity of the sentence structure and added a redundant sentence. Use of overly complex sentences can emerge from undergraduate writing advice that varied sentences 'keeps the reader interested'. However, you do not need to rely on the writing to keep the reader interested because your research will keep them engaged. Therefore, use simpler sentences containing one or two statements where you can. There will be instances in your writing where it is not possible to do this, for instance, if you are providing a fairly rigid definition or listing clauses. Save the complex sentences for the times where they are needed, so the reader will not become bogged down in the writing.

Writing redundant sentences is one of the most common errors in academic writing. This is where you state the same information but in slightly different ways. It often comes from an anxiety that the reader needs some further clarity. If you have this feeling, instead of stating the same information differently, go back to your previous sentence and check it against the other technicalities we have covered. Respond to the need for clarity by reiterating key words, building from simple to complex information, and simplify your sentences. This will prompt you to strengthen the clarity of your writing and will save your reader the labour and confusion of reading sentences that provide no new information.

All of these techniques represent good academic writing generally. Use them particularly to prepare your paper for a Q1 journal so that your research is communicated with absolute precision and clarity. The more quickly and clearly your research and its importance can be understood, the more it is suitable for the wider audience of Q1 journals. Considering all of these factors, when writing for a Q1 journal you should aim for a writing style that authoritatively states one clearly novel conclusion in a way that a non-specialist audience can understand.

Develop your writer's ear

Now that you understand what Q1 journal editors are looking for and have explored some techniques for effectively communicating your research, one final activity will help the long-term development of your writing for this audience. Wyse (2018) has referred to the 'writer's ear' as being similar to a musician's ear, arguing that writing follows similar patterns to written music: 'the sense of intonation, for music and for written language, particularly facilitates the editing of words and sentences until they reflect the author's intended meaning' (2018, p. 220). Wyse's allusion to writing as music here serves as a reminder that formulae alone will not write a Q1 paper. Indeed, while all Q1 papers share a common formula of authoritative and clear writing that can be understood by a wide audience, the other feature they have in common is that they are truly original, cutting-edge and different. This cannot be achieved through a formula alone but comes from your engagement with your own research and the story you have to tell from it. Wyse suggests that 'the ear of the writer is a part of *inhabiting* the world of the writer, as well as the more technical act to "read like a writer"' (2018, p. 219). Tune your writer's ear to writing for Q1 journals by reading articles not just from your own discipline, but also from other disciplines.

It can be difficult to identify good writing in your own discipline because you will read to understand the research rather than to consider the writing. To combat this, set aside half an hour each day to read the title, abstract, introduction and conclusion of two or three articles from Q1 journals outside your discipline. You do not need to examine them carefully or deconstruct their writing techniques. By simply exposing yourself to written research outside your field, you will develop your awareness of the common features of writing across Q1 journals. This will help you to improve your writing in the long term and to increase your vocabulary and confidence in expressing the story of your research with clarity and authority. While the writing techniques and advice in this chapter should act as your guide, use them in conjunction with tuning your own 'writer's ear'.

Once you have finished preparing the first draft of your paper, use the editing checklist below to hone your writing. Remember that first drafts of any writing will not be perfect and, even with the best intentions when writing, you will probably find multiple points where you can clarify or simplify your writing. When your paper is ready for submission, congratulate yourself. Make sure that you rest and forget about the paper while you wait for feedback. Your paper will either be passed on for peer review or you will need to re-prepare the paper for your second-choice journal. Both require energy, so it is important that you have had a break from it so that you can re-engage with this process once you get to this stage. Top Tips 5.1 summarises our advice for successfully publishing in a Q1 journal.

Top Tips 5.1

Publishing in Q1 journals

1. Forget about the terminology. No one has ever sat down to 'write a world leading paper'.
2. Focus on communicating one clear message as clearly and widely as possible. Follow the activities in this chapter to help crystallise your main conclusion and why it matters.
3. Download two to three articles from different disciplines per day to 'tune your ear' to the style of writing in Q1 journals.
4. Use SJR or other bibliometrics to explore the ranking of journals in your field.
5. Draw up a list of four Q1 journals that you cite in your research as they are likely to be more relevant to your paper.
6. Start with your preferred journal. Follow their guidelines closely when preparing your paper.
7. Refer to the guidelines in this chapter for authoritative, clear and concise writing when preparing your paper.
8. Do not submit to more than one journal at a time.
9. Do not worry if your paper is rejected. In 2017 *Nature* published 7.6% of the papers it received for submission. Congratulate yourself for having the confidence to try.

(Continued)

10. Move on to the second-placed journal on your list. Prepare the paper using *their* guidelines; do not give them an easy reason to reject you.
11. If your paper undergoes peer review, take the revisions seriously. Copy and paste each comment from the reviewers, and write below it where and how you addressed this change in the paper, referring to page numbers.
12. Writing a quality publication is a marathon, not a sprint. Focus on the revisions stage or re-preparing for a new journal; otherwise, you are likely to spend considerable time trying to make your original paper 'fit' new criteria and burn out.

Finally, while this is a process that demands time and effort, it does so because it is worth it. If you would like to share original research with a wide audience, you too can be part of this world even if it feels intimidating at times. We hope that the guidance in this chapter may help you to engage with and enjoy the process.

Further reading

Bishop, K., Gruys, K. and Evans, M. (2018) Sized out: women, clothing size, and inequality. *Gender and Society*, 32(2): 180–203.

Freeman, D., Reeve, S., Robinson, A., Ehlers, A., Clark, D., Spanlang, B. and Slater, M. (2017) Virtual reality in the assessment, understanding, and treatment of mental health disorders. *Psychological Medicine*, 47: 2393–2400.

Lau, S.S.Y., Zhang, Ji. and Tao, Y. (2019) A comparative study of thermal comfort in learning spaces using three different ventilation strategies on a tropical university campus. *Building and Environment*, 148: 579–599.

Lipscy, P.Y. (2018) Democracy and financial crisis. *International Organization*, 72: 937–968.

Walters, R.K., Polimanti, R., Johnson, E.C., McClintick, J.N. et al. (2018) Transancestral GWAS of alcohol dependence reveals common genetic underpinnings with psychiatric disorders. *Nature Neuroscience*, 21: 1656–1669.

Wyse, D. (2018) *How Writing Works: From the Invention of the Alphabet to the Rise of Social Media.* Cambridge: Cambridge University Press.

6

How can you publish books and chapters?

Guest author: Patrick Brindle

This chapter examines how you can go about publishing academic books and book chapters. It covers how to:

- Decide when and whether writing a book or book chapter is right for you
- Work out what kind of book it will be and for what specific audience
- Target publishers and write successful outlines and proposals
- Engage with your intended readership

Getting an academic book or book chapter published requires a different set of skills compared to writing and publishing journal articles. The key players in the process are different. For instance, while much depends on your capacity to select the best target journal for publishing your article, for book publishing the challenge is more about identifying the best publisher for your work. Getting a book published involves going through more iterative stages than getting an article published, but often those stages are managed more efficiently by publishing professionals who can normally give you feedback at each stage about what is required and how long everything might take. Importantly, you need to understand that the main gatekeepers who decide whether your work is publishable are the publishers rather than your peer reviewers.

In this chapter we will work through the typical stages of coming up with a book idea, getting it approved by a publisher and then writing for publication. We will keep the focus general to encompass different types of academic books, including edited books, textbooks, professional books and 'trade' books. In Chapter 7 we will turn our attention to how you can turn your doctoral thesis into a 'monograph' and so we will avoid talking too much about that topic here. Of course, there are many points of overlap in the process regardless of whether you are interested in publishing your thesis in book form or writing an introductory textbook for students.

Reflection Point 6.1

Know what makes publishers tick

It is important to understand how publishers work and what publishers are looking for if we want to get our ideas published in book form. That means understanding that publishers are commercially-driven actors and will seek to evaluate each proposal not only on its academic merits but also in terms of its suitability for the market and on its likelihood to make a profit (or at least not make a loss). A good publisher will always seek to maximise the commercial or market advantage of a book, so their feedback needs to be understood with this in mind.

Deciding whether a book is the right idea

Writing or editing a book can take a long time. It can be a big commitment in terms of your energy and resources. Therefore, it is important that you are clear from the start why you want to write or edit a book and that it is the right thing for you to do. In many disciplines, and in many countries, there is an increasing preference for academics to write articles for high impact factor journals, and this is particularly the case in scientific, technical, engineering, mathematical and medical (**STEMM**) fields. If you are considering writing a book chapter, while it may not represent the kind of scale of undertaking as doing a whole book, your colleagues may wonder why you are not submitting your work as a research paper to a journal instead.

There can be very good reasons why writing a book or book chapter might still represent a very good choice. First, many kinds of academic book, with the likely exception of a monograph, can find a larger or more diverse readership than most journal articles, thus connecting your ideas and work more widely within and outside academia than most journal articles can. Further, books also provide you with more space and more freedom to unpack ideas without squeezing them into the shrinking word limits of journal articles and can often give you the space to find your own voice.

Evidence is also emerging that some types of book, specifically research methods books, also receive higher citation levels than even the top-ranking medical and scientific journals (Green, 2016). After all, most research publications need to cite methodological literature and so books about methods receive huge cross-disciplinary exposure.

In some disciplines, most notably in some of the humanities, a particular kind of book, be it a monograph or other kind of academic book, remains essential to build one's career and indicate academic esteem to one's colleagues.

In deciding to write or edit a book, you will probably be seeking a contract with a well-known and recognised academic publisher. Part of the process of deciding whether a book is the right option for you involves asking honestly whether you are planning the kind of book that an academic publisher is likely to want to publish. If you are thinking of writing or editing a densely argued 150,000-word opus on a niche topic, you need to be aware that it is highly unlikely that a recognised academic publisher will want to offer you a contract. Such books are nearly always rejected by publishers. The Reflection Point 6.2 will provide some reasons why this is the case.

Reflection Point 6.2

Will anybody actually buy your book?

Ask yourself will my book sell? Publishers will not offer to publish your book unless they think it will sell enough copies to break even. Seriously consider who will buy your book and what evidence do you have that similar books have been successful?

Sadly, if your primary reason for writing an academic book is to make money, you are probably misguided. A small handful of textbooks and 'trade books' will earn their authors a nice sum of money, but such books represent only a very tiny fraction of the thousands of academic book titles published each year. To make a serious financial return on your book-writing investment you need to produce a book that will sell tens of thousands of copies per year. However, you may have other motives, such as improving understanding of a topic, so you will want to know how you can improve the chances of your book being published.

Before we move on through the next stages of the process, it is necessary to offer some important advice to would-be academic book authors and editors: **ALWAYS make sure you get a contract first before devoting too much time to planning and writing the manuscript** because publishers rarely publish unsolicited manuscripts. Indeed, from a publisher's perspective it is easier for them to shape the process and improve the development of a book while it is in its infancy. Working from a long existing manuscript to reshape and reinvent a project is often a thankless and dispiriting experience for publisher and author alike. Do not give up, though. Consider the Information Box 6.1.

Information Box 6.1

Reasons to be cheerful

Working 'backwards' from an existing long manuscript may be difficult and dispiriting but working 'forwards' from an initial idea or proposal can be a much more rewarding and well managed process. Good commissioning editors are available to bounce ideas off in a way that a journal editor seldom is. The peer-reviewing process for academic books will be quicker and probably more extensive than for your research papers, and when reviewer feedback is confusing or contradictory the editor will be a willing and helpful interpreter and arbiter of the feedback.

What kind of book will it be and for what publisher?

One of the assumptions we are making in this chapter is that you will want to write or edit a book for a recognised academic publisher. The peer review process that underpins academic publishers' decision to publish book proposals and manuscripts confers upon authors a similar badge of academic legitimacy and kudos as is found in serious peer-reviewed journals. Of course, there are many spaces online where researchers can self-publish books, chapters or, indeed, research papers. However, self-publishing seldom comes with the badge of legitimacy associated with peer review and with passing the quality control criteria of serious academic publishers. Further, self-published books will not benefit from the marketing and sales support that can make books more visible to a global academic audience. To get a recognised academic publisher's buy-in to your idea you will first need to have a really good idea of what kind of book you want to write or edit.

Finding the right publisher for your book idea

Different publishers specialise in different types of book for different markets. For instance, Pearson, Cengage and SAGE mainly publish textbooks, and each will have different discipline strengths and weaknesses. Oxford University Press and Cambridge University Press also publish textbooks, but in some fields will accept monographs and 'trade' books. Your challenge is to work out what publishing house is the best for your book idea. That means knowing what each publisher wants and represents, but also knowing what kind of book you want to write and knowing that the type – or 'genre' – of book is acceptable to that publisher. At this point, working through Activity 6.1 will help you find a suitable publisher.

Activity 6.1

Identifying appropriate publishers

There are a number of rough-and-ready strategies you can use to help you with this task:

- Start by doing a web search for books on your general topic. Draw up a list of the publishers who keep recurring in your search and cross-off from your list of possible publishers any who do not feature in your search results.
- Supplement your web search with a similar exercise on your library website and on Google Scholar, making sure to filter your results for book content only. Again, look to identify the names of the frequently recurring publishers in your search.
- Once you have a shortlist of possible publishers visit their company websites and try to work out whether they are still actively publishing a range of books in your field. If you can, try to find out whether a 'commissioning editor' or 'publisher' is assigned to commission books in your discipline, because this will indicate an ongoing commitment to the field.

There are other factors you should think about in deciding on the right publisher for you:

- **Personal rapport with your editor**: Do they 'get' your idea? Will they be your advocate and offer good advice along the way?
- **Ambition, activity and commitment to the field**: Is the publisher operating in the area for the long term, rather than just dipping a toe in the water?
- **Sales and marketing reach**: Can your publisher do things to promote your future book with the market and readers that you envisage the book being for?
- **Prestige**: Will your colleagues be impressed and recognise the academic status of the publisher? Remember, publishing your 800-page opus with the **Vanity Press** will not impress fellow scholars.
- **Territorial reach**: How important are overseas sales and language rights? Can your publisher secure you a deal with a foreign language publisher and is it important that they do so?

No two academic publishers are alike. Each has different specialisms, publishes a different genre mix and has different strengths and weaknesses. Perhaps counter-intuitively, your task as an author is not to spot the gaps in a publisher's list, but instead to target the publisher that already publishes the books that most closely resemble the book you are planning to write. To explain, SAGE has established strengths in publishing social science books, research methods books and professional texts, but does not publish monographs, poetry or fiction (see Top Tip 6.1). Your manuscript may represent the next great novel of the 21st century or the greatest contribution to plant biology in a generation, but SAGE will still not be able to publish it because it does not have the capacity to market such books.

Top Tip 6.1

Do not oversell your idea

Many authors try to finesse the question of what kind of book they are writing by claiming in their proposal that their book is a mix of many genres appealing to a mix of markets. This is a mistake. By claiming your book will 'appeal to academics, students and the general public; that it is a serious, yet accessible book, that could be used for course teaching and to move the discipline along', you will seriously lessen the credibility of your proposal with the publisher.

Identifying the kind of book you want to write

Finding the right publisher therefore involves being clear exactly what type or genre of book you wish to write, not blurring those genres, and then developing a rubric for the book that is a close fit with what typically the publisher wants. Crudely, the most common genres of academic book are as follows:

Monographs: Normally a published and re-written version of a doctoral thesis or single body of original research. The intended readership is small, consisting largely of fellow scholars in the same field.

Textbooks: Written to support student learning, most commonly to support a course. Where courses are large, the publisher will want the book to represent a very close match to common course content to secure 'adoptions' of the text to support a course. Textbooks exist at various levels, from school texts, undergraduate ('core' or **'modular'**) texts, to higher-level (**'supplementary'**) texts. If a proposed textbook does not represent a good fit with common course content it is likely to be rejected.

Reference and student reference: Dictionaries, encyclopaedia and glossaries count as 'reference', while books on study skills and on practical academic skills also fall into this category. This book is probably best categorised as 'academic reference' because, unlike a textbook, it is not geared to a course, but instead looks at a range of practical skills researchers might need to develop their careers.

'Trade' non-fiction: 'Trade' books are written for the general public through retail channels such as high street bookstores and Amazon. Such books need to be accessible and assume little or no prior knowledge of the topic. History and

Popular Science are the two biggest 'academic trade' markets, and notable 'trade' authors might include Mary Beard, Richard Dawkins and Antony Beevor.

'Professional' books: In some fields academic authors often write 'professional books'. These are written to support professional practice in areas allied to academic research, such as nursing, law, medicine, social work, school teaching, and so on. Such books are accessible and practical in tone and are nearly always closely tied to an element of professional practice. They are intended to be read by professionals rather than by students.

Other types of academic book: There is a great deal of diversity of type of academic book, and some types of book are harder to squeeze into neat categories. Handbooks, for instance, are edited volumes seeking to capture the state-of-the-art in a specific academic field. They are large, edited by big-name academics and contributors are similarly expected to be stars or rising stars. Other books blur the textbook boundaries, being written somewhat for students but also for academics to move thinking in one direction or another. At the other end of the spectrum, Wiley produces 'For Dummies' titles and Oxford University Press has its 'Very Short Introductions' that blur the trade, reference and textbook genres.

All the above genres can be authored, co-authored or edited.

Authoring versus editing?

An early and critical decision you need to make is whether to author, co-author, edit or co-edit your book. Sometimes this is an easy question to answer. If you are turning your doctoral thesis into a book, then it almost certainly will be a sole-authored enterprise. Similarly, if you are planning a very large-scale reference book, you will need to edit or co-edit the work to realistically cover everything required of such books.

For many books, the decision to author or edit would appear to be less clear cut. There are pros and cons to both approaches.

Authored and co-authored books

The most straightforward way to produce an academic book, providing it is not too long and does not plan to cover too many areas, is to author a book. Authoring gives you control over voice, style, features, content, theory and argument, and declares the book to the world very much as *your* project and *your* contribution to scholarship. However, if you find writing to be a very slow process or a painful one, and you know realistically that writing anything of book length will take too much from you and take too much time, you may wish to consider co-authoring.

Co-authoring with one or two other people can, when the project goes well, dramatically decrease your workload and can sometimes be a fun and rewarding experience. However, selecting the right co-author is key. Differences in voice, style, vision, expectations, speed of delivery or even of personality can lead to friction and stress. If you are considering co-authoring, we advise you to consider some of the tough questions we pose to those of you considering editing a book and applying them to a potential co-author as a means of working out whether it is the best approach for you. You may also find it useful to consult our sister book, *Success in Research: Inspiring Collaboration and Engagement* (Reeves et al., 2020).

Edited books

We need to be clear from the start that editing a book is rarely an easier option than authoring. On first impression it would appear a less daunting task to sub-divide your 100,000-word manuscript into 10 chapters with each chapter having its own author. That is an achievable 10,000 words each, right? Your calculus is right in theory but is often wrong in practice when it turns out to be harder than you expected to commission 10 different authors, harder still to get each author to deliver on time, and harder again to smooth all the rough edges of 10 separate manuscripts each with its own voice, level and overlapping and underlapping assumptions. Most academic publishers will tell you that they prefer authored and co-authored books. Publishers are much more likely to see a final manuscript of an authored book, while too many edited books never get delivered to the publisher at all (never mind 'on time').

Edited manuscripts that are delivered often need more work done to them before they are ready for publication. More repetition needs cutting, and more stylistic and level differences need smoothing. It is your job as editor to make sure this is done. Some submitted chapters may need root-and-branch rewriting, or, worse still, may require that you eject a chapter outright, with all the stress and diplomacy that entails.

To make editing work for you, it is important that you are realistic about what to expect and that you are not doing it because you think it is the easiest way to produce a book. You need to be prepared to be a tough editor at times, and to expect and plan for lateness, non-delivery, sub-standard delivery and substantial rewrites and stylistic smoothing. Be prepared to ask authors to revise and re-submit their chapters, regardless of who they. Be prepared to ask contributors to leave the project if need be, regardless of who they are. Can you do that?

If you are going to edit your book, the selection of your contributors is key. Pick who you think will be the best contributors to the book, rather than who your friends are or who your boss happens to be. Try to avoid issuing a call for chapter contributors and instead be an active editor by handpicking contributors against honest and tough selection criteria. Are they able to write:

- In the style you want
- For your target audience
- To the quality you need
- Within your specified time frame?

Realistically, how much trouble and work are you storing up for later when you must edit, intervene, cajole and nag the individuals in question?

Information Box 6.2

Checklist for selecting contributors – honestly – as an editor

- I trust this person to deliver on time
- I trust this person to write well enough for the intended audience
- I trust this person to take on board my feedback positively (even if that is bad news)
- I trust this person to write what I ask them to write (rather than something random that they happen to feel like writing)
- If it comes to it, I know I can have a difficult conversation with this person about their work
- If it comes to it, I know I can remove this person from the project
- I am not even a little bit scared or intimidated by this person
- Nor do I feel sorry for them, there is no way this is an act of charity
- I have honestly ticked all the boxes above (yes, really).

If you decide to take the edited route, you need to extend your 'active editor' role beyond the commissioning process into the management of manuscript writing and delivery. Your watchwords here should be communicate, communicate, communicate. Do not simply abandon your contributors for months on end without regular communication and hope that all manuscripts will deliver nicely on deadline. Instead, ask for progress reports, request draft chapters, seek regular updates. Fully brief each contributor on exactly what is expected. Tell them or explain/set out in person or on the phone, not on email:

- Who the book is for
- What it is seeking to achieve
- The role their chapter plays
- The level required

- The features required
- What your role as an editor will be
- The consequences of late or non-delivery, and
- Prepare them for any editorial interventions that may be needed.

If you plan to co-edit a book, remember that you can be amplifying the challenges or halving them, depending on your choice of co-editor. Ask yourselves difficult questions about whether you can work together. How you will work together? How differences of opinion might be managed? What will the shared vision for the project be? A good co-editor is a friend, ally and sharer of your workload, but the wrong choice of co-editor could make the challenge harder, not easier.

Be clear-eyed about what you are writing or editing

To repeat, it is unwise in your proposal to state that you are blurring the boundaries between different types of text. Publishers want authors to produce the type of book they know will sell and that they can market. Even those genres, such as 'For Dummies', that do blur boundaries, do so with their own tried-and-tested format and expectations. Thus, something that is a bit 'monography' and a bit 'For Dummies' is unlikely to be of interest to most publishers.

Before you start to write your proposal, get a sense of the market. Get to know how the books look in your chosen genre: the style they are written in, who they are aimed at, the features they have, how long they are. Find out what competition you have and think about what your book can offer that others do not. Ask colleagues or students what they find useful in a publication covering the area you want to write in. All this knowledge needs to inform the development of your proposal.

Writing an outline and the proposal

When you know what type of book you will be writing and you have identified a handful of likely publishers for your book, the next stage is to make first contact with your target publishers to outline your ideas. If you wish, you can visit the publishers' websites at this stage and write out a full proposal and send it off, cold-calling fashion, to the relevant 'commissioning editor'. We would advise, however, that a better approach might be to resist writing a full proposal (something that takes a lot of time, research and thought to be done properly) until you have first made contact with a publisher/commissioning editor to get initial buy-in. Information Box 6.3 will help you address the right people.

Information Box 6.3

Job titles in the publishing world

Understanding who does what in publishing can be confusing. For example, when we refer to a 'Publisher', we can mean the publishing house (or company) or the name of a senior person in the editorial department in charge of some of the book lists. So, the word 'publisher' can refer to a person or a whole company. 'Commissioning editors' – sometimes called 'acquisitions editors' – do largely the same job as 'publishers' (the people) but are normally more junior within the organisation. For your purposes, it probably does not matter whether you write to a 'publisher' or a 'commissioning editor' or 'acquisitions editor'.

Presenting an outline of your idea before drafting a full proposal is a good idea. If the commissioning editor says 'no' to your idea, it can be disappointing but can save you a huge amount of time and energy. You can walk away from the idea now or ask how the idea might be improved to make it more publishable. If their advice seems do-able to you and is not alienating, you can accommodate those changes in your proposal, which will already be more likely to get an approving reading from the publisher. You can present your outline in an email or as an attachment or verbally on the phone. You can even do so in person if you know you are going to an event or a conference which the publisher will also be attending. Your outline should be short, informal and informative. It is not a document that will ever be peer reviewed, so do not worry about citations and references at this stage.

Top Tip 6.2

Do your homework

If you are emailing your outline, always write to a named person rather than 'Dear Sir or Madam' or 'To Whom it May Concern'. Writing to a named person shows you have done your research and that you are taking the process seriously.

A good outline should be no more than two or three pages in length and should make a pitch for why it would be a good idea for the publisher to publish the book. Your audience is one person at this stage: the commissioning editor. Set out, clearly and persuasively:

- The rationale for the book
- Why it is needed

- Why it will be successful
- Who it is for
- Why they will buy it
- What is its Unique Selling Point (USP)?
- Its place in the market (*vis-à-vis* the competition)
- A **synopsis** of what the book will cover.

A good editor will then be able to give you honest feedback based on their assessment of whether the proposed book will work as proposed in the market. Unlike some peer reviewers, publishers rarely let their own personal feelings about the research approach or theories deployed in the book shape their sense of whether the book is suitable for publication. You now need to work with the editor's feedback (if you feel you can). Listen to their advice and start to build an editorial relationship with the publisher if it feels right to do so. Think about how comfortable you are about the editor's feedback; are you happy accommodating their suggestions, or is it moving the project too far in unintended directions? If the vibe does not feel right, consider going to a different publisher. This stuff really matters. Your relationship with your editor is potentially a long one, so it is important that you work well together. That is why it is important to learn from rejections as well as enthusiastic encouragement. We provide some advice on that in Top Tip 6.3.

Top Tip 6.3

Turning rejection into a learning experience

If the editor says they do not like your outline or proposal, ask:

- How can it be improved?
- What other publisher would be best to sound out with such a proposal?

Try to get the fullest and most honest feedback.

Writing the proposal

If the commissioning editor likes the outline, they will ask you to submit a formal proposal. Invariably, publishing houses will have proposal guidelines and sometimes a proposal template available on their websites. It is a good idea to draft your proposal to follow closely the guidelines and template. If you are proposing a textbook, trade book or handbook, your editor should be willing and able to share suggestions with you on how to perfect and draft the proposal, and you should feel confident about asking for feedback on any proposal drafts you submit.

Some, although not all, publishers will ask for a sample chapter to accompany your proposal. However, check the guidelines, because if a writing sample is not requested, you could slow the process up while you spend weeks drafting something that is not required. You might wonder if you could save time by sending your proposal to more than one publisher. We discuss that in Information Box 6.4.

Information Box 6.4

Can I send my proposal to lots of publishers?

Compared to submitting journal articles for peer review – where you cannot submit your article to more than one journal at time – you have more leeway with a book proposal. You are entitled to send your proposal to as many publishers as you wish. However, it may not always be a good idea to do so. Most academic books make very little money and if a publisher has already invested time in your project, they may feel cheated if you take their advice and tout it to all bidders.

Bear in mind also that if more than one publisher elects to send your proposal to review you could be faced with the embarrassment of the same academics being asked to review the same proposal by two separate publishers. Unless you know you are writing a genuine bestseller, it is probably best to settle for sending only your outline to multiple publishers and then selecting only one publisher to handle the proposal itself.

Your proposal needs to provide an account of the contents of your proposed book, its potential market and its relationship to other books in the market. It is written to impress both the publisher (and their colleagues in the company, such as sales managers, marketing managers, and so on) and the academic readers who will be selected as peer reviewers. Thus, it has a dual and contrasting target readership and needs to make sense for the commercially-minded publishing house readers and the academics who will evaluate your proposal in terms of its **contribution to knowledge** or its utility as a teaching text. As well as a synopsis of the book and its argument/approach, you will be asked to provide a table of contents (or 'ToC' or 'tee-oh-cee') containing a good paragraph of information on the likely contents of each chapter.

You will also be asked by the publisher to comment on the market for your book. It is never a good idea at this stage to write something along the lines of 'You are the publishers, you tell me about the market!', because that is to misunderstand the purpose of this section of the proposal. By asking you to assess the market, the publisher is checking whether your plans for the book are realistic, whether you know the competition and have a way of dealing with it, and that you have a clear idea of who you are writing for and what they need. Your publisher is just as interested in your interpretation of the market and the competition as they are in the proposed contents of the book. Remember, it is 'buyership' not 'readership' that a publisher is really interested in, so explain who will need the book enough to buy the book and what the likely numbers and location of these people around the world might be.

Always detail the competition (and relate it to your own book's merits). Explain why a reader should buy your book and not another book. Never write in a proposal 'There is no competition for this book' because, (a) there is *always* competition, and (b) you have again misunderstood the purpose of this information for the publisher, who will want to benchmark your proposal against the sales and market strategy of the nearest similar book. Set out the strengths and weaknesses of your competition honestly, charitably and in full. Your publishers and reviewers will know the competition, so do not be unfair in your evaluation. Do not simply say 'Competitor book X is rubbish' because the book is likely to be known and used by your reviewers (and perhaps the book's author may even review your proposal). Set out how your book intends to be different and better than the competition in realistic and reasonable terms. Do this in relation to reader needs and market conditions.

Peer review

If the commissioning editor likes your proposal, they will send it to **peer review** to get academic backing for the proposal. Depending on budget, and the type of book it is, you can expect to have anything between two and 12 academic reviewers assigned to review the book. Unlike peer reviewing journal articles, most book proposal reviewers are given strict deadlines (weeks not months) to complete their review. Comments are always varied, and it is the publisher's job to synthesise and present the reviews to you, advising you on feedback they think is valid and requires action and on what comments they feel can safely be ignored or discounted. It is the publisher who makes the final decision about whether to offer you a contract or not, and they weigh up the reviews in tandem with their own costings and market analysis to come to a final decision about whether to proceed.

At this stage it is common for the publisher to ask you to redraft your proposal a little in response to the reviewers' comments or at least to state how the book will change to accommodate the most pertinent feedback.

Your revised proposal, along with the reviews and a whole raft of editorial and marketing information put together by your publisher will then be used to make the case at an editorial meeting for you to be offered a contract. The contract will set out the parameters of the book (its coverage, length, features, etc.), the financial deal (your advance, if any, and royalty rate) and the deadline for delivery of your final manuscript. Now you have the small matter of writing the tome.

Writing your book

You will be sent author guidelines packed with information on the publisher's house style and delivery requirements. It is important, if you want to avoid further unnecessary work down the line, that you follow the guidelines closely, share them with any co-editors or co-authors and submit your manuscript in the format requested. Your contract will stipulate a delivery date and your planning process will need to be geared to being able to deliver the manuscript on time.

Academic publishing has become increasingly seasonal to fit with sales cycles and term dates, so missing your deadlines could present serious problems for the publisher seeking maximum uptake of your book. Missing deadlines also dents your reputation with your publisher and could potentially lessen your chances of your next proposal being viewed favourably. However, academics missing deadlines hardly constitutes front-page news, and if you really are unable to deliver your manuscript on time, it is much better to give your publisher advanced notice of the likely delay. In preparation for receiving your manuscript, your publisher will be organising production teams and marketing campaigns, and so leaving it until your contracted deadline day to inform your publisher that you need another three or six months to deliver not only makes you look bad but undermines the many preparations being made for your book.

Sometimes you may be asked to produce drafts of chapters at specific times, so that your publisher or peer reviewers can evaluate the quality and audience-suitability for your work.

The writing task

Writing anything, whether it is a book, book chapter, or journal article, can often feel like a daunting prospect. It is not unusual for would-be authors to find the writing process painful and hard to conquer. One way to make the task more manageable and less scary is to understand that you are not writing for yourself, but rather you are writing for a specific audience to communicate a finite set of ideas, findings or arguments *only for that audience, in terms that the audience will best understand.* All academic writing is an act of communication with another group of readers and is not your cue to cover every base from every conceivable angle with differing degrees of sophistication. You are writing for a specific group of real people. Ask yourself:

- Who am I writing for?
- Why are my readers reading my book?
- What do they need to know?
- What do my readers know already?
- What needs further explanation, contextualisation and justification?
- How can I be most meaningful and convincing in the eyes of my readers?

To help you focus on this, consider the idea in Top Tip 6.4.

Top Tip 6.4

Write for real people

To really viscerally grasp who your readers are, and to focus your mind on communicating clearly with that audience, find a photograph of a person or persons typical of your target readership. Stick this photograph close to your computer screen. Each day, before you start writing, spend a few seconds looking at the picture to get you in the communication zone.

The style and level of your writing will inevitably vary hugely depending on the type of book you are writing and your intended audience. Textbooks, for instance, will almost certainly require that you supply a range of 'pedagogical features' – such as learning objectives, case studies, activities, questions – to enhance the readers' learning experience. Your publisher will advise you on what kind of 'pedagogical features' to include. Lots of academic books that are not text-books increasingly also come with in-text features to make them more accessible, including boxed features, bullet lists, sub-headings, summaries, and so on.

As a rule of thumb, when writing books and book chapters, your publisher will expect you to write in a more accessible style than you would in your PhD thesis or in a typical journal article. Books are still expected (in fact are commercially required) to find a larger audience and so your target readership needs to be realistic yet broadly conceived. For a textbook, it is relatively easy to profile your target readers; you are writing for student learners on a specific course with the intent of helping them learn all that is required of them to get through their course. For more general academic books aimed at your fellow researchers, you still need to reach out to a broader audience than your immediate research sphere. In your specialist field there may only be a few dozen active scholars – not nearly enough to represent a viable book market – so the publisher will expect you to write your book in such a way that scholars and researchers in a reasonable number of adjacent fields will also be interested in the book and will also find it understandable and meaningful.

If you are writing a 'practitioner book' remember that your audience will comprise busy professionals seeking practical advice they can deploy in their own work. So, ease off on the history, theory, philosophy and methodology when writing for teachers, nurses, social workers and other practitioners. Use language that they will understand, and when jargon or complex language is unavoidable take the time to explain it, perhaps including a glossary, particularly if your audience is international. Often different terms are used for the same thing (cf. dissertation and thesis in the UK and the USA) or a term means different things to different groups (cf. doctoral **viva voce** in different European countries).

Co-authoring

Many books and journal articles are co-authored. What co-authoring means in practice varies enormously. In some STEMM fields, it is not unusual to encounter research papers with dozens of author names listed. In such cases, the actual writers of the manuscript comprise several individuals from the larger research team who, by virtue of their participation in a large-scale research project, all count themselves as authors. In the humanities and social sciences, it is unusual to encounter dozens of named authors on a publication, and instead the assumption is that the two, three or four listed 'authors' have all had a hand in the actual writing as well as in the research. Thus, it is probably useful to differentiate between co-authoring (where lots of people have their names listed as authors) from co-writing (where individuals work together on the words and sentences themselves).

If you are considering whether co-writing is the best approach for you, it is important to first understand it as a strategy that can bring considerable risks as well as considerable benefits. The potential upsides of co-writing are many:

1. The work is shared and so the workload and pressure may be much reduced, and the time taken to finish the work may be shorter.
2. Good collaboration can be intellectually and analytically fruitful, spurring new ideas, syntheses and insights that can enrich and power-up your publications.

3. Less experienced or less confident writers can learn craft skills through working with more experienced or confident colleagues.
4. Opportunities arise to play to a team's strengths – one of you may be good at infographics and data analysis but less good at phrase-making or writing for audience, but together you have all bases covered.
5. Many research projects are themselves collaborations, and the data and theories to be generated from the research are themselves the result cooperative intellectual labour.

There are, however, significant risks to co-writing. Like any relationship, some combinations of people work well together, and others do not. It is not always possible to know in advance whether you will work effectively with a prospective co-writer, but if you are already wary of the prospect, you may wish to heed the warning signs. In the worst cases, close friendships and even romantic relationships can be broken through unhappy experiences of co-writing. If you have different sets of expectations, different notions of what you are trying to achieve, different work or writing styles, or even non-matching timetables, co-writing could become much more difficult than simply writing it all yourself.

A good co-writing experience requires high levels of alignment between all those involved on a range of parameters, and that means from the beginning working out between you where you stand on the following issues *vis-à-vis* the book or chapter you are about to write together:

1. *Intellectual alignment.* Are you all happy and agreed about the arguments you are making, the data you will deploy, the examples you will use, the connections you will make, and so on?
2. *Stylistic alignment.* Can you agree a style and a process for smoothing the style so that all parts of the book are in keeping with each other in terms of level, voice and vocabulary?
3. *What will be the actual writing process?* Will you sit and write together on the same computer? Where and when will this happen? Will you send each other drafts for the other to amend? By what dates? Who writes and who edits?
4. *Who has the final say?* Sort out the power relations. Disagreements will always arise, but do you have a mechanism for settling them? Who ultimately decides? Get this sorted from the very beginning of the project.
5. *Who will be the first named author?* In many fields it matters to be first. Do not leave it to the end to decide whose name is listed first. Consider whether an author should 'earn' the right to be first listed by doing more of the research and writing on the project?

Co-authoring can be a great way to be a more productive author, but you should always get the parameters agreed from the start of the process. All those involved need to be ready to compromise to make the experience a success. Writing is always a highly personal thing – even academic writing is partly about us revealing something of our identity or inner self – and that is why co-writing can sometimes be so fraught with risk and high emotion when the process starts to go wrong.

Writing a chapter for an edited book

The chapter you are reading now is a contributed chapter for a book. My job as a contributor has been to follow the brief set by the book's authors and try my best to match the style, features and level of writing set out in the guidelines to contributors. The editors will have agreed the guidelines beforehand with the publisher.

Most chapters for edited books are written by invitation. The editor decides in advance who would be a good candidate to write on each particular topic and allocates topics accordingly. If you are going to write such a chapter, you need to know as much as you can about the expectations of your editor for your chapter's coverage, level and style of writing. You should also look at the proposed table of contents to make sure that you are not covering topics being dealt with elsewhere in the book by other contributing authors.

Some stylistic easy wins

There are many excellent books on writing for academic audiences (see Further Reading at the end of the chapter) and we do not have the space in this chapter to revisit the full range of how-to-write advice found in those books. Our point is to stress to you the need to understand that your book writing should always be audience focused, that your concept of audience needs to be broadly conceived, and that your writing needs to be meaningful, explanatory and convincing for that audience.

There are some stylistic easy wins that you should consider using in your book writing. Indeed, some of these easy wins can just as happily be deployed when writing journal articles.

Vary your sentence length: It is a myth that you should always look to write in short sentences. Unless you are writing a very short-form piece, such as an abstract or blog, one of the best ways of adding power and elegance to your writing is to vary the length of your sentences. A good mix of shorter and longer sentences adds rhythm and flow and is much easier to read. Good novelists know this instinctively. Be careful, though. You should still look to cut out very long sentences in excess of 40 words because they are hard to follow.

Deploy shorter paragraphs: More and more of your readers will be reading your work online, either on a computer screen or a mobile phone screen. Paragraphs that appear to go on for many pages are tiring to read and off-putting. Without being too rigid about it, try to keep your paragraph length to within a range of 8–20 manuscript lines.

Use more sub-headings: Similarly, on-screen readers, and probably readers of print too, will welcome the text being broken up occasionally with helpful sub-headings. Again, you should not be robotically adding sub-headings at overly regularised intervals, but instead should consider using a clear, descriptive sub-heading as frequently as appropriate every four to eight paragraphs.

Build bridges with your examples: One of the most common goals of writing academic books is to educate your reader; taking them from a position of not knowing (much) about something to knowing (a lot more about it). To help readers grasp what was previously unknown to them we need to use plenty of 'for examples', 'for instances' and 'in other words' to illustrate any issue we feel our readers will need more help with. Such examples need to be meaningful to your reader, so achieve this by seeking parallels – by building bridges – between similar familiar examples and the new thing you are seeking to explain.

Self-narrate: Occasionally in your manuscript you should be prepared to self-narrate your text. By this we mean you should explain clearly and succinctly what each section of your chapter is doing and why it is important your reader should read it. For instance, when writing about your research design you should consider explaining to your reader why it is important to grasp the key elements of your research design before they go on to read about your results.

Using jargon: The use of technically or theoretically specialist language – jargon – is often regarded as a bad thing when writing books because it can confuse and alienate readers who are unfamiliar with the terms. But saying all jargon is wrong badly oversimplifies and misrepresents your task as a book writer. Imagine instructing trainee surgeons on how to do brain surgery without using the necessary terminology for the different parts of the brain and equipment required: *Cut open the patient's head, find a sharp tool and remove the bad bits*. Precision in language is vital, clearly. More problematic is when jargon is used not for precision but to show off or obfuscate and when a more accessible word or phrase would not surrender any precision. For instance, if we used the word 'dishabituated' instead of the word 'homeless' we are probably open to accusations of not writing clearly and accessibly.

Your book writing should be clear and vivid, yet precise. Good writers are aware of exactly who the audience is and make the necessary adjustments to bring them along for the ride. We think it helps too if you can inject a sense of warmth and enjoyment in your writing. Be persuasive by imagining that you are writing for a specific group to communicate some interesting, meaningful, important and compelling things about your topic.

Voice of Experience 6.1

A successful book author's tips

1. Do not be a perfectionist and forever rewrite drafts. Submit early and treat referees' comments as gold dust. Now you can see what might be required to make your way in the academic world. If your re-submission is not much better received, you probably have only yourself to blame.
2. Reviewing the pros and cons of an accepted approach can be like trying to reinvent the wheel. Keep as much space as possible for your own arguments.

David Silverman is the author and editor of many successful textbooks, including *Doing Qualitative Research* (SAGE) and *Interpreting Qualitative Data* (SAGE). He is series editor of the *Introducing Qualitative Methods* books for SAGE.

Key things to remember

In this chapter we have looked at how you can go about deciding whether writing a book or editing a book is a good option for you, examining the pros and cons of editing versus writing a book. We have also started to explain how you can identify the best potential publisher for your work and examined how and when to approach them to give you the best chance of securing a contract. We also made a start at setting out a few hints and tips about how to embark on the writing process.

We have stressed that the process of getting a book accepted for publication is quite different from how you go about getting a journal article accepted. The biggest difference is that the main gatekeeper at a commercial publisher is the commissioning editor. To get them on board, we noted how it is nearly always better to present that person with a condensed outline of your book idea, while it is probably a bad idea to write an entire manuscript before approaching a publisher.

Our advice to you when writing an outline, a book proposal and indeed a chapter or the book manuscript itself is basically the same: remember you are never writing for yourself but writing to communicate with an identified readership. At each stage, therefore, consider your readers first when deciding what to include and omit from your writing.

One final reminder, if you publish a book with a commercial publisher and it is a success, you better get ready to write or edit new editions every few years because a good publisher is always looking for a new edition. Good luck.

Further reading

Denicolo, P.M. (ed.) (2014) *Achieving Impact in Research*. London: SAGE.

Elbow, P. (1981) *Writing with Power*. Oxford: Oxford University Press.

Green, E. (2016) What are the most-cited publications in the social sciences (according to Google Scholar)? https://blogs.lse.ac.uk/impactofsocialsciences/2016/05/12/what-are-the-most-cited-publications-in-the-social-sciences-according-to-google-scholar/

Holliday, A. (2007) *Doing and Writing Qualitative Research* (2nd edition). London: SAGE.

Kousha, K. and Thelwall, M. (2018) Can Microsoft Academic help to assess the citation impact of academic books? https://arxiv.org/ftp/arxiv/papers/1808/1808.01474.pdf

Osmond, A. (2013) *Academic Writing and Grammar for Students*. London: SAGE.

Reeves, J., Starbuck, S. and Yeung, A. (2020) *Success in Research: Inspiring Collaboration and Engagement*. London: SAGE.

Richardson, L. (1990) *Writing Strategies*. Newbury Park, CA: SAGE.

Strunk, W. and White, E.B. (2000) *The Elements of Style*. Boston, MA: Allyn & Bacon.

Sword, H. (2012) *Stylish Academic Writing*. Cambridge, MA: Harvard University Press.

Thody, A. (2006) *Writing and Presenting Research*. London: SAGE.

Wallace, M. and Wray, A. (2011) *Critical Reading and Writing for Postgraduates*. London: SAGE.

7

How can you turn your thesis into a book?

Guest author: Christian Gilliam

In this chapter, you will be introduced to:

- The differences between a thesis and a monograph
- The how and why of rewriting and restructuring a thesis for publication
- The process of selecting a publisher and writing a book proposal
- The publication process, from submission of the proposal to the publication of the book

The definition and purpose of a monograph

When we talk about turning a thesis into a 'book', we are really talking about a **'monograph'**. 'Monograph' is a Latinised compound of the Greek word μόνος (*mónos*), which means 'alone' or 'single', and γράφω (*gráphō*), which simply means 'writing', hence, the Latin *monographus*, as in 'to write on a single genus'. In keeping with the etymological sense of the word, a monograph is generally considered a written work that focuses on one specialised subject with a view to contributing original insight and knowledge. Therefore, a monograph is to be contrasted with a **'reference work'**, which is something concerned primarily with conveying basic information such as dates, names and terms, and a 'textbook', which is concerned with surveying the state or history of knowledge in a specific field (see Chapter 6 for ideas on how to write and publish these kinds of book). Given that a doctoral thesis – particularly in the arts, humanities and social sciences – is a dedicated study on one specialised topic or area of research, it stands to reason that it is a kind of proto-monograph. What we are concerned with in this chapter is the way we turn your proto-monograph into a fully-fledged and published monograph.

Why speak in terms of 'proto'? Could the doctoral thesis be published as a monograph *as it is*, with little or no changes? We suggest not. Although both outputs share a detailed and dedicated content, the aim and audience of a doctoral thesis is distinctly different from that of a monograph. This results in a distinct difference in both the *form* and *style* of the work. The primary aim of a doctoral thesis is to achieve a qualification and title, and its primary audience are the academic examiners of the viva voce. As with any qualification, this means there are certain criteria that must be met to the satisfaction of the examiners. Chief among those criteria is that of an 'original contribution to knowledge'. Underlying this, as a somewhat more tacit and unofficial criterion, is what we can call 'researcher verification', where the academic worth and ability of a doctoral researcher is verified through his or her thesis. Thus, a doctoral thesis has: (1) a descriptive and expository element to it, a sort of 'look what I know'; (2) a degree of preliminary groundwork in the setting out of an argument and justification of method; and thus (3) an element of *hyper-justification*.

With a monograph, such extra detail is surplus to requirements for both the aim and the audience are different. The aim is not to confer a title which indicates specialist skills and knowledge, but rather to contribute to and disseminate knowledge to a wider audience, through a recognised and peer-reviewed medium. Therefore, the audience, though still *relatively* educated, will not be as specialised on the subject nor as concerned with academic verification as examiners. The monograph is pitched to an intelligent general reader in your subject area, who is interested in the *argument* and its relation to and/or effects on the subject area; the reader is not interested in *you*! If you were writing a monograph on the political theorist John Rawls' concept of justice, for instance, you would want to reach out beyond political theorists purely interested in Rawls, for that is a relatively small audience. We consider next how to achieve that 'reaching out' to a broader audience.

Rewriting and restructuring

We have just established that the thesis is designed to communicate your ability and credentials as a researcher, whereas the book is designed to communicate an idea or an argument to a wider audience and research landscape. With this general rule in mind, it is necessary to reconsider and adapt the overall narrative and structure of the work. We can break this down into several finer points. First, locate and refine the central argument of the work. You might, for example, be offering a specific, and hitherto neglected, interpretation or aspect of John Rawls' concept of justice. The central argument should be, or is likely to be, the most captivating aspect of the work itself. If the central argument is not captivating or of interest, then why set pen to paper, fingers to keyboard? Why is what you have to say worth saying? Ultimately, you are asking yourself: 'why am I so passionate about this?'

Second, consider the broader impact or the significance of the central argument. Do not preach to the converted, that is, do not write solely for readers in your specialist field or academic circle. If you do this, your central argument will be too subtle and nuanced to be of any use or interest to your wider audience. The purpose of a monograph is to connect and communicate both to *and beyond* your circle. To return to our Rawls example, a monograph may be concerned primarily with a specific hitherto-neglected aspect of his concept of justice, yet the broader point is likely to be that the work challenges the whole concept of justice, which would be of interest to both political theorists and legal practitioners alike. In this way, the work goes through its subject matter in order to go beyond it. This relates to the 'so what?' question. How would you answer this question in a way that would garner the interest of the readership? Therein lies the captivating significance of the work. This is what you want to highlight, especially in the introduction and conclusion of the work. This would be a good point to engage in Activity 7.1.

Activity 7.1

Distilling the essence of your thesis

Often thesis examiners, having read through your thesis in detail, want to be sure that your findings are not simply novel, but are also non-trivial and worthwhile. They want to hear your defence that your work will have impact of some kind: theoretical, economic, social, etc. They therefore ask the 'so what?' question. We suggest that you formulate an answer to that same question in relation to your argument but as if you are being asked by a parent or friend. How would you convince them of the value of your research? What is its relevance in or to their lives? How would you capture their attention?

Introduce the captivating aspect as early as possible in the text itself. This follows a general rule followed by most journalists: draw the reader in at the start. In terms of converting your thesis into a monograph, this simply means: start where you end. A thesis starts on some form of question that itself must be justified through a heavy engagement with, and analysis of, the relevant literature (that is, 'verification', as discussed above), methods and data (if applicable). A book starts with the answer.

A monograph can afford to be, and indeed is encouraged to be, more **polemical** than a thesis. Steer away from impersonal, technical, dry and abstract academic writing. Try to avoid the jargon of your specialist field but, where unavoidable, find a way of using such jargon that is intelligible to a non-specialist. As part of this, you may wish to consider using an active tense and personal pronouns where appropriate, for example, 'I argue that Rawls' concept of justice is incompatible with free market economics'. (See Chapter 5 for more about this style of writing.)

In addition to the writing style, you will find it helpful to revisit the overall structure and organisation of chapters. While the prospect of restructuring may be daunting, you will find that in practice it is highly liberating. With a monograph you are free(er) to be creative and rewrite the thesis outside the formal constraints. That is, you can give your distinct voice and textual-character more freedom than it had in thesis form. Do not get too lost in creativity, however. Your *primary* aim here is to find and employ the most seductive and persuasive way to structure, and therefore present, your work. You need to carry the reader along, provide them with a clear path to follow and keep them wanting more. In some circles/countries this is known as either the red or golden thread that leads you through the forest of complexity.

Restructuring will involve relegating peripheral material to footnotes, or even deleting them entirely. There is a lot of expository groundwork that goes into a thesis, including a detailed engagement with the literature, methods and analysis of data. The thesis requires the student to display their overall understanding of the subject and the related issues and concepts involved. Such work is designed to confirm to the examiner that you hold a good understanding not only of your specific area of research and adjacent fields, but also of the *process* of research itself in its more holistic or 'meta' sense. As you can imagine, such groundwork is superfluous in a monograph, and its inclusion will only serve to take up valuable space and perhaps bore or irritate your reader.

Those particularly familiar with your field (your academic circle) will already be aware of the literature, theoretical developments and the matter of method, while those outside your field (the broader academic audience) will find such discussions irrelevant to their interest. The former people are looking for something that will push the academic envelope within your niche, whereas the latter are looking for something that will contribute to knowledge in the wider sense. Neither of the two are seeking a *tour de force* of the field, nor an audit trail of your data and method. This means that each chapter needs to add something new and argumentative in a way that, when taken together, will communicate your main argument. Restructuring goes a long way in explaining why monographs tend to be shorter than theses, with the former being on average around 60–80,000 words and the latter around 90–110,000 words.

You also need to construct a terse and cogent text from beginning to end. Get straight to the point and stick to it. Apparent deviations are permitted on the premise that they necessarily and intelligibly serve the point; that is why the deviatory character is only 'apparent'. A good polemic is no substitute for substance. The polemic should serve to complement the substance of your argument. See this as an amplification of the essence of your work that will allow it to be heard. The quality, in other words, is still required to be of a sufficiently high level.

We now turn to a question that must be asked of yourself before you commit to such an endeavour. Why do you think it would be beneficial for you to turn your thesis into a monograph? What are you hoping to accomplish? There is no right answer as such, but it is important to be clear about what you aim to achieve, and whether this is a practical and realistic undertaking. Writing a monograph is a lengthy process that requires commitment, patience and resilience.

Although writing a monograph can be very fulfilling, it is not to be taken lightly. First, there is some important groundwork to do, not the least of which is interesting a publisher by preparing an attractive proposal. We turn to that next, although you can glean something important about the perspectives of publishers in Chapter 6 too. One point highlighted in that chapter is the importance of preparing an outline and talking to potential publishers to solicit their interest in receiving a full proposal before you actually draft the full proposal. Chapter 6 also provides ideas on how to select publishers who might be interested in your monograph. See specifically Activity 6.1 and then consider the advice in Top Tips 6.1 and 6.2 and Information Box 6.4. Once you have eliminated publishers who have other foci and raised some interest in your monograph project, then start to prepare your formal proposal.

Selecting a publisher

Choosing a publisher is much like choosing a university. Some will be well-known and will draw enthusiastically raised eye-brows when mentioned, although this does not necessarily mean they are right for you or appropriate/respected in your field. Others may be less well-known but more suitable to your purposes. Of course, you will need to define what those purposes are. If it is for strictly academic purposes, then naturally you will wish to ensure your publisher has a proven track-record in your field, and that they are respected as a high-calibre source for knowledge among your peers, with a good selection of titles. (See Chapter 6 for some ideas about the specialisms of publishers.) For better or for worse, academic work is easily judged according to what it is associated with and, in this context, **university presses** tend to be a good match. Conversely, if you are trying to reach as wide an audience as possible, **commercial presses** will be preferable as they are better equipped at marketing and will likely sell your book at a reasonable retail price.

As a rule, university presses come with prestige, whereas commercial presses come with wider dissemination. There are of course exceptions to this, but it is easy to see why aiming for a large audience would necessitate the watering down of content such that it may compromise its academic novelty. That does not mean to say commercial presses are interested exclusively in popular books or 'trade non-fiction'. Many commercial presses specialise in academic monographs and offer excellent opportunities to early career researchers seeking to publish their thesis.

Our advice is to look at respectable titles in your field to see who they publish with. This will give you some good ideas about which publishers to approach first. Be sure to ask the advice of your supervisors and fellow researchers too. You may also have a case for going for an alternative or lesser known publisher, based on political, **ethical** or financial grounds, for example, if they support open access. Whatever your choice, be sure to avoid 'vanity presses'. A vanity press publishes scholarly monographs on a print-on-demand basis. The author is usually required to pay for the editing, production and distribution of the book. The peer review process and quality of editorial services are also of a low standard or entirely non-existent.

The proposal

Not only will a formal proposal be required by a publisher before they can agree to publish your work, it will also help you flesh out and refine the rewrites and revisions you will need to make. Most publishers will have a proposal template available on their website. For the most part, they all follow the same structure, with some minor variation. Therefore, you can either write a more general pro-posal according to a general structure, or write initially according to a specific publisher's template, with a view to adapting it for another publisher should that be required. The point is that the templates hardly differ, so that once you write one proposal you are unlikely to have to make any drastic changes when (or if) submitting to a second or third publisher. Below we list the various sections of a typical proposal, with a brief explanation of each.

Title. To begin with, you will need to choose a title. Publishers are keen to avoid clashing metadata (data about data), so you should avoid replicating your thesis title. You are likely to want to do this anyway, as a thesis title is normally quite dry, long and overly technical. A good title is essential for marketing your book. A good, marketable title is short and clear about the purpose or subject of the monograph. A subtitle can be included if you wish to add a little more detail about the contents of the book. At least one keyword should be included in the title that will facilitate its **discoverability**. Think of terms or words likely to be used by your target audience in search engines.

Synopsis of aims. You are likely to be asked to set out the aim of the proposed book. Even if you are not asked this, it is a good exercise to set it out because it will help you clarify and define the project and, above all, help you to distinguish it from its thesis form. The synopsis should also include a discussion of the subject area of the book, the approach you intend to take, the structure and style, and themes, concepts and ideas developed. A good place to start in developing the synopsis is with the abstract of your thesis. Do not replicate the abstract, but rather use it as a springboard from which to develop the synopsis.

Key features and benefits. You may be asked to provide a brief bullet-pointed list of the distinctive qualities and benefits of your book. Again, even if you are not asked to do this, it is a worthwhile exercise in that it will further help clarify to yourself the worth of the book. The key features should expand upon the captivating aspect of your argument, as mentioned earlier. For example:

'10 case studies explaining different aspects of sociolinguistic variation to clarify your understanding of the subject'

'Sets out an innovative agenda for liberal democracy, opening new avenues for your research'

'Based on primary sources, including newly discovered records from the European Court of Justice'

'Offers a fresh theoretical and methodological perspective on communicative behaviour'

Chapter-by-chapter description of content and form. You will need to provide a list of chapters, along with the main sub-headings. Each chapter should be accompanied either by an outlining paragraph and/or a short sentence or two for each sub-heading summarising the content. You may want to include a list of the key authors, texts, case studies or examples covered by that chapter. Provide an estimated word count for the chapters, if possible.

Suitability. You will probably be asked to state your intended academic audience. For example:

First- and second-year undergraduate students

Upper-level undergraduate students

Postgraduate students

Academics, scholars and researchers

Market and readership. You should outline the markets your monograph will reach. The main factors to consider here are national and cultural boundaries and relevance, for example, whether it is marketable within and/or outside the UK; the primary readership, for example, postgraduate students studying political theory; the subject area/s your book will appeal to, for instance, political studies, sociology and philosophy; and the courses your book could be used for, for instance, introduction to political ideas (cite actual university courses if possible).

Competing and comparable books. Contrary to what you may believe, stating that there are no comparable books will not speak to its originality and so will not be viewed as a strength of the proposal. A publisher wants to be assured that there is a pre-existing market for your book and that it is relevant to the literature of the field. With this in mind, list between three and five competing or comparable books published in the last five years. Competing books are on the same subject that people might buy instead of your book, whereas comparable books are on a similar subject that people might buy as well as your book. Competing and comparable books should be of the same book type (for example, monograph, textbook) and aimed at a similar readership. When citing books, be sure to include the title, author, publisher, publication year and price. Above all else, ensure that you briefly outline what distinguishes your book from the competing and comparable titles, that is, why people should buy your book instead or as well, which is an important issue in marketing your monograph. For further help with discovering potential markets, engage with Activity 7.2.

Activity 7.2

Some guidelines for marketing your book

Below are our guidelines for researching the market of your book and how to market it. These are suggestions and are by no means exhaustive.

1. Search online to look at what courses are on offer that relate to your field. In what way would your monograph contribute to the course? It may offer something

different for an undergraduate and a master's course. Create a spreadsheet of courses identified, including the name and contact details of the course convenor and/or the library collections team.

2. Search online and ask colleagues to identify scholarly associations and/or professional organisations in your field. Will your work appeal to them or be of any use? Would they be able to provide a review of your book? Most publishers can provide pre-published sample copies of your book for review purposes. As with the above, create a spreadsheet including this information necessary for your own reference. This will make it easier to track who you have contacted, who has replied and who requires a copy of the book. The publisher may want this information too.

3. Assuming that you have researched the related literature in sufficient depth, you should already have a pretty clear idea of what competing and comparable books presently exist. Indeed, you should be able to identify competing books by first referring to your own bibliography. Check online via Google and/or Amazon using key terms to identify any recently published works that have not been included in your research. Remember, as a general rule, you should only select books published in the last five years.

4. Consider the broader marketability of the book. Are your competing and comparable titles available in other countries? Any countries in particular? If yes to one or both questions, it is worth considering why that is and whether the reason is applicable to your work. This could potentially help pitch your proposal to the publisher and increase sales.

5. Create a spreadsheet with the publication details (author, year, publisher) followed by a short synopsis and an outline of how your book differs. This may also help you to identify the key features of your book.

6. Once the book is forthcoming, use your spreadsheet to contact the libraries and/ or universities you identified as offering courses on subjects related to your field (or course leaders where appropriate). Speak with your publisher to see if you can provide a sample copy for the course leader.

7. Once the book is published, embark on a social media campaign. Use media like Twitter to advertise the title and share links to related pages, blogs and reviews. Encourage your friends and colleagues to leave reviews on retailer webpages, such as Amazon.

A curriculum vitae. A CV will give a quick outline of your credentials and thus capacity for producing your proposed book to the desired quality and within a reasonable time frame. Be sure that your CV includes details of any relevant experience and a list of any previous publications (books and/or articles).

Other supporting materials. Be sure to include any other materials you feel can be put forward to illustrate the proposed approach and/or demonstrate your writing experience and ability, for example, a draft chapter of the proposed book and a list of competing titles or articles written by you on the same or a similar topic. That said, many publishers will require a writing sample of sorts anyway, so be prepared to provide one.

As indicated in this section, there is a lot of preparation to engage with before you begin the actual process of writing.

Selecting reviewers

As with all academic work, a monograph is peer reviewed. Unlike a journal article, you are usually free to choose or at least recommend your own reviewers, in much the same way as you and your supervisor chose examiners for the final assessment of your thesis. Indeed, the considerations for both are usually somewhat similar, that is, you want to select reviewers knowledgeable of the field and sympathetic to the nature of your project and ideas. Supervisors are not generally accepted as viable reviewers, because of an obvious conflict of interest. You will need at least two reviewers, although it is recommended that you list four or more in case any of the reviewers are not free to accept the request. Requests will be dealt with by the publisher, for purposes of anonymity – which is another reason why a publisher will ask for more than two reviewers.

Decision I: Commissioning editor/series editor

Once you have prepared your proposal and selected your potential reviewers, it is time to contact the **commissioning editor** of your selected publisher. This is likely to be the person whom you interested with your outline. Most publishers have a commissioning editor for each identified subject area, for example, Philosophy, Politics, Psychology, Sociology, and so forth. So be sure to select the correct editor. Contact them, as detailed in Chapter 6, providing all relevant information. They will then decide whether your proposed monograph still fits within the strategic vision and publishing strategy of the publisher. If it does, the proposal will then be sent out to review with the aim of confirming the quality and novelty of the proposal, along with supplementary material such as the writing sample. The reviewers may suggest some changes to the proposal that the editor will insist on before they commit to sending it to the editorial committee. As with any review process, pay careful attention to what is recommended and make sure you are comfortable with the changes. This is *your* book after all!

Decision II: Editorial committee

Once satisfied with the proposal, the commissioning editor will present it to the publisher's editorial committee. Such committees tend to be comprised of academic advisors, fellow commissioning editors, a member of the marketing team and senior editors. A multitude of aspects will be considered as part of the decision-making, including marketability, suitability for the publisher and its strategic vision, and academic novelty. The committee is likely to meet once a month or even once a quarter, so there may be an element of waiting at this stage. The commissioning editor should inform you about dates and time-scales.

Contract

If your proposal is approved by the committee, you will be contacted by your commissioning editor with the outline of a contract. As with any contractual arrangement, it is crucial that you carefully read through the terms and ensure you understand and agree with them. Feel free to ask for clarification and pay extra attention to any submission dates. Dates can usually be changed, especially if you feel that the proposed submission dates do not give you enough time to complete the manuscript to a high quality. It is better to be clear at the beginning with yourself and the publisher than to accept out of excitement only to find yourself overwhelmed later down the line.

With respect to pay, the typical arrangement is payment via **royalties** (payment from sales) of around 3–6% of sales profit, without an advance. There may be different arrangements for the hardcover and paperback prints. Some publishers will only commit to printing the hardcover edition, with a promise of a paperback edition should the publisher sell a certain number of units. Bear in mind, too, that the retail price of the hardcover is likely to be significantly higher than the paperback. Search for recently published titles in your field to get a clearer idea of the average retail price.

The writing/reviewing/editing process

The start-to-finish process of publishing your monograph is longer and more tedious than at first imagined by most first-time authors. Time-scales vary, but on average you should expect to go from proposal to publication anywhere between one and two years, possibly even longer if this is your first foray into book writing. Be sure that you factor this in when planning your workload, especially if you are embarking on your post-doctoral career, which will probably be an adventure into the unknown. We address the various stages of the process below. The order is linear, although it should be borne in mind that the order of the process can, and does, vary; where there is a rule, there is always an exception!

The bulk of the work in this process is yours. You will need to write and rewrite the monograph according to the feedback given by the reviewers. If you are publishing as part of a series, the series editor will expect to see drafts to ensure you are keeping within the remit and style of the series. In any case, you will need to frequently review your work and edit it to ensure that it is clear, grammatically correct and devoid of typographical errors. The publisher should give you some guidance on effective self-editing and reviewing.

Free feel to pester colleagues and friends to review your work, although ensure you acknowledge them in the preface or acknowledgements sections. Most academic writers are fully aware from experience of the many drafts that lay between first ideas and the final, polished version so will probably be willing, especially if it is a reciprocal arrangement, to scan your drafts. Friends may be less willing, but they are an important 'lay' resource to tell you about how accessible your writing is. Perhaps a promise of a dinner or similar might be an inducement.

Deadline I: Final manuscript

You will be writing to a final manuscript deadline. The manuscript refers to *your* version of the work. This is likely to be reviewed internally, giving you and the publisher one last opportunity to revise sections that are unclear and/or cumbersome. Once this is done, the manuscript will be sent off for copy-editing.

Deadline II: Copy-editing/indexing for final transcript

Copy-editing, which is usually done through a third party, focuses less on the contents of the argument and more on the technical aspects of the writing, for example, typographical errors, punctuation, spelling, grammar, and so forth. The copy-editor is likely to return the copy-edited typescript with several queries concerning proposed changes to spelling and syntax where the meaning is in question.

Some changes will not be queried even though they significantly change the meaning of a word or sentence. This usually results from the use of terms that are not recognised in common English and/or from ambiguous sentence structures that, although clear in meaning to you, may have another sense or meaning to the copy-editor. In other words, what you may see as correct, they may see as incorrect or unclear. In addition to this, copy-editors and publishers tend to use a software called **LaTex** for typesetting. Converting from a Word document to LaTex can cause formatting errors that affect punctuation and spelling. It is crucial, then, that you read through the typeset proofs in detail to check for any additional errors. This is best done by printing the work off and reading through it assiduously with a pencil ready to hand. Tedious though this is, it will save you from potentially embarrassing mistakes.

Be aware also that there are specific symbols used in proofreading that you will likely have to utilise when addressing queries from the copy-editor and proofreader. These are either physically inserted onto a hard copy of the typescript or digitally inserted onto an electronic copy. You will be guided by the publisher on the use of such symbols at the time and the way you are to return the annotated pages.

With respect to indexing, few publishers offer free indexing services. Indexing is usually quite expensive for first-time authors; therefore, it is likely that you will want to do this yourself. It can be time-consuming, but again the publisher will provide instructions on how to do this. There is an advantage to doing it yourself, as you will have the ultimate say as to what words, terms and/or names are indexed because you will/should know what words are important and likely to be sought in an **index**.

Marketing

Once copy-editing and proofreading is completed, the book will be sent off for printing. While in preparation, the publisher will embark on a marketing campaign. Some publishers are better than others in this respect, so ensure that you are aware of what is being done and be prepared to get involved. It might be worth organising a book launch, embarking on a social media campaign, contacting university libraries and book reviewers, and blogging. See Chapter 10 for some ideas. Irrespective of how you choose to market your book, let the publisher know of your plans. Not only will this avoid duplication of work, they may also be able to offer assistance and perhaps provide flyers.

Publication/post-publication marketing

The first task here is to bask in the glory of your achievement! Getting a book published is a monumental achievement and one that you should readily recognise. Of course, there is still some work to do. You should remain active in promoting your book. Again, you can do this by sending your book out for review, writing blogs about it, offering talks or a publication launch party and contacting libraries and relevant course convenors. Of course, then there is the next book proposal to think about!

Further reading

Germano, W. (2013) *From Dissertation to Book* (2nd edition). Chicago, IL: University of Chicago Press.

Harman, E., Montagnes, I., McMenemy, S. and Bucci, C. (2003) *The Thesis and the Book: A Guide for First-Time Academic Authors*. Toronto: University of Toronto Press.

Luey, B. (ed.) (2007) *Revising Your Dissertation: Advice from Leading Editors*. Berkeley, CA: University of California Press.

Melbourne University Press (n.d.) *Turning Your Thesis into a Book*. Online: www.mup.com.au/blog/turning-your-thesis-into-a-book (last accessed 11/10/2018).

Palgrave Macmillan (n.d.) *Advice from our Editors: Revising the Dissertation into a Monograph*. Online: www.palgrave.com/gb/why-publish/early-career-researcher-hub/revising-the-dissertation (last accessed: 11/10/2018).

8

How should you write for lay audiences?

In this chapter you will:

- Learn about the various benefits of lay publication for you and your research
- Think about which lay audiences you may want to communicate with and what key messages to communicate
- Consider the variety of different lay publishing opportunities available and how to choose the best options for your research
- Discover how writing in a clear, jargon-free way need not mean 'dumbing down'
- Explore how the writing structure and content of lay publication differ from traditional academic publishing

Why write for lay audiences?

Before we address how to write for lay audiences, it is important to consider and explore why you would want to consider writing for this audience type. In Chapter 1 we discussed motivations for publishing and highlighted the importance of publication to create academic, economic and societal benefit. For research to have an impact on the world it has to be shared, and publication is the vehicle for this. In Chapter 2, we explored different audiences for your publication and thought about how to attract different groups of people to your work. While it is likely that the main target audience for your publications will work within academia, it is also quite likely that there are audiences outside the academy who are stakeholders in your research. They may be stakeholders because they work in areas that would benefit from understanding your research to improve processes, drive innovation or influence policy. They may be stakeholders because understanding your research would help them, or those they are caring for, live better lives. They may be stakeholders simply because their taxes, in part, pay for your research. All of the above are reasons that a lay audience may be an important target audience with whom you should communicate your research.

Lay publication is a powerful tool for this type of communication, because it is easier to reach a large audience with written publication than by holding an event or giving a talk. Of course, lay publication requires an investment of time, not only due to the effort in crafting the writing, but also because of the need to develop the specific skills necessary to communicate effectively with a lay audience. Because of this investment, it is worth considering the benefits to this type of publication for your research and for your career.

Increasingly, the writing of lay statements, lay summaries and lay abstracts is becoming embedded within requirements for funding proposals and for some journals, particularly large open access ones (see Chapter 9). Therefore, the first practical reason for learning how to write for lay audiences may be to secure funding to support a project which you can then write about for the academic journal of your choice. For some researchers, the first response to such additional requirements is to bemoan yet another hoop to jump through that takes time away from the 'real job' of doing research and communicating with fellow academics. However, we suggest you ponder the reasons why these requirements are becoming widespread.

Funding bodies and journals are asking for these sections because they believe they are important for ensuring the research they fund or publish is as widely understood and used as possible. Funding bodies have an interest in demonstrating to the public who fund research through their taxes that their investment is sound and results in valuable research. Writing a clear summary, in a way that is accessible to all, promotes transparency and highlights the importance of research.

Thus, lay publication may lead to a greater use of research both academically and non-academically. There is now evidence that writing for lay audiences increases citations (Liang et al., 2014; Kuehne and Olden, 2015). Communicating with different public audiences can also lead to eventual economic, societal and cultural benefits, as demonstrated in the UK Research Excellence Framework (REF) **impact case studies** (see Chapter 12).

Some of today's most pressing scientific, societal, environmental and economic issues are being addressed by researchers around the world. Communicating with different public audiences helps to ensure that relevant and potentially impactful research is not left out of the conversation when policy makers address these issues. Writing academic-facing publications is not enough to ensure a broad range of people will access and use research, because these types of publication are not readily accessible to the general public, practitioners or politicians who might utilise it. Voice of Experience 8.1 presents a small collection of academic accounts of the personal and professional benefits of lay publication.

Voice of Experience 8.1

Personal and professional benefits of lay publication

The following quotations are from a range of published sources in which academics discuss their experiences with lay publication.

In an article for *The Conversation*, Dr Amy Schalet (2016), from the University of Massachusetts, made a case to include this type of writing in tenure considerations, citing her examples:

> In my own work on adolescent sexuality, culture and families, I have found that my articles for general audiences resulted in much greater visibility for my academic publications. What was most rewarding was that I found a way to reach parents with information that could improve their relationships with their teenage children.

Within an article in *The Guardian*, Dr Kim Yi Dionne expressed her surprise at the impact her blog had:

> That one blogpost generated academic opportunities, an academic article, a scholarly book chapter and, indirectly, a National Science Foundation grant. It was such a catalyst. (Brent Zook, 2015)

Demonstrating the benefit of lay writing for professional skill development, Wai and Miller (2015) state in an article for *The Conversation*:

> We don't think we are amazing writers, but we do think writing for the public has helped us improve. The immediate feedback from editors and the public has helped make our writing clearer. ... We've learned that if we're not clear and engaging, then editors and the general public simply won't read us. And that continues to teach us how to improve the next time we write.

The experiences in Voice of Experience 8.1 demonstrate the link between research and professional impact and lay publication. In Reflection Point 8.1 we ask you to think about the impact of such public communication within your academic field.

Reflection Point 8.1

Lay publication in your field

Do you know of researchers in your area who write lay publications? How influential are they within the academic context? Do you think that lay publication has had an impact on their academic success, whether this be in terms of esteem or in terms of academic citations? Do you find the academic writing of these authors to be of a high quality?

As discussed further in Chapters 11 and 12, both academic and societal impact take time and, therefore, should be seen as the longer-term goals of your writing activities. However, there are plenty of short-term benefits to be cultivated as well. One such benefit that we discuss in our sister book, *Success in Research: Inspiring Collaboration and Engagement* (Reeves et al., 2020), is that the public you are communicating with can become collaborators in (or at least contributors to) your research. By writing for wider audiences, the reach of your work extends, the likelihood that someone who reads your work and is interested in it increases, and the pool of ideas generated becomes deeper. Information Box 8.1 summarises a range of potential benefits to you and your research which may arise from lay publication.

Information Box 8.1

Potential benefits of lay publication for you and your research

Lay publication:

- Expands your network
- Increases your ability to successfully gain research funding
- May increase citations
- Confirms or legitimises the importance of your research
- Provides access to more participants
- Enables potential recognition by industry or donors
- Could lead to innovative ideas for future projects
- Accesses a larger pool of collaborators
- Provides a gateway to people with specific expertise
- May increase student recruitment
- Prevents others from misinterpreting your research
- Could lead to greater non-academic impact or potential impact case studies
- Leads to professional recognition and esteem
- Enhances your writing ability

As evidenced by the mass consumption of a range of information sources online, the public has a great desire to consume information. Providing the public with high-quality, evidence-based information not only empowers the public to make good decisions for themselves and their loved ones, but also may enable them to make advances on a wide variety of challenges that different 'publics' are tackling in their daily lives. Making research accessible means making it available openly (see Chapter 9) as well as making it understandable and useable. Additionally, by giving the public a platform to respond to, or comment on, your work, you can provide an avenue for them to have an influence over future research directions. In this way, lay audiences can move from being passive consumers of information to active participants in driving research agendas focused on topics that are important to them.

Planning your lay publication

Now that you understand why lay publication is important and impactful, it is time to start thinking about planning your writing. In many ways this is similar to planning any publication. As discussed in Chapter 4, when planning your publication, the first thing you have to think about is what you want to communicate – in other words, what the key message is that you wish to convey. Then you can consider who the best audience is for this message and what type of publication is most likely to reach them. However, there are specific considerations in terms of message, audience and format that are unique to lay publication.

Your audience

In Chapter 2, you were asked to think about the various people who may be interested in your work. We encouraged you to think beyond academia and consider people with a variety of different backgrounds. For the purpose of this chapter, it is important to consider the diversity of lay audiences you can target. 'The public' is not one homogeneous audience, but actually a collection of many different 'public audiences', from different backgrounds, professions and personal situations. Therefore, it is important to think about what public audience would be interested in your work and, possibly even more importantly, as discussed further in Chapter 12, what public audience could best contribute to your work (see Voice of Experience 8.2).

Voice of Experience 8.2

Learning from the public

As a researcher, I had been involved in communicating my research to various public audiences for many years; however, it wasn't until I started truly listening to the public that I fully understood the power of public engagement. At the time I was researching a specific disease. Of course, I had read thousands of papers about the disease. I had also read incredibly sad clinical histories of patients who had donated their tissue to help make a scientific breakthrough. Despite all of this knowledge, it was in listening to the lived experience of patients and their carers that I gained a greater appreciation for what my data was telling me and impacted my future analysis and interpretation of my results.

This insight has given me a new appreciation for two-way engagement with the public, and for the opportunity that researchers have today to reach out to public audiences that have unique and important views on the subjects we are researching. We live in a time when this type of engagement is becoming increasingly possible on a larger scale. Publishing a lay article in an online magazine or blog can provide the public with information about your research, but they can also invite comment, ideas and participation. As researchers, we just have to be humble enough to ask for this input and to listen. Trust me, there is great benefit in doing so.

A neuroscience researcher

Once you have identified which lay audience you are intending to reach, it is important to understand their point of view. Activity 8.1 is designed to help you start to reflect on your audience and their perspective on your research area.

Activity 8.1

Getting to know your audience

Knowing how and where to pitch your work for a general audience can be challenging. Before you start writing, ask the following questions about your audience:

- What do they know?
- What may they not know?
- What do they care about?
- What may be surprising to them?
- What might capture their attention?

If you do not know the answers to these questions, it is worth investigating further, either by talking directing to people who make up this audience or by talking to people experienced in engaging with this audience; they may be publishers or other researchers experienced in this type of publication or your university **press office**.

If you find you are struggling with Activity 8.1, it may be important for you to do more research on your audience before trying to write for them. Engaging in discussion with members of the audience is the ideal way to do this. For example, if your research has potential implications for medical practice, it is a good idea to talk to medical practitioners and patients; this will help you hone your publishing for this group to make it even more impactful (see Chapter 12). Once you have identified your audience and understood their perspective, it is important to focus your key message to match their interests.

Your message

In Chapter 1 you thought about various key messages you wanted to communicate, so you probably have an idea of the message you would like to write about. Now, it is important to tailor this message so that your target audience is interested and engaged with your publication. In general, lay audiences care much more about why you are doing your research and why it is important than how you did it. In simple terms they want you to answer the question 'so what?', rather than 'how?'. Lay audiences are not interested in the detailed information that typically appears in an academic methodology or methods section, or the long historical background of the research leading up to your findings. They want to understand exactly how your research will make their lives, or the lives of the people they care about, better. When planning a lay publication, you must think about what the audience you are reaching out to wants, or needs, to understand. This is the key message to focus on.

Your publication format

Once you know your audience and the key message you want to convey, it is now time to think about the best format to publish it in. While this is a seemingly simple question, with the multitude of possibilities, it requires careful consideration. Below we list some of the more common types of platform for non-academic publishing along with their pros and cons.

Lay summaries or abstracts: Although not usually a publication in their own right, lay summaries or abstracts can draw broader audiences to your work. When writing them, it is important to think of the broadest audience possible and make your work accessible to them. Emphasising the impact or potential impact of your work is of critical importance.

Magazines and newspapers: These types of publication are a great way of spreading the word about new research or providing commentary on a topic in general. Magazines typically are more area- or topic-focused, aimed at their subscription audience, while newspapers tend to have broader content, although often with a particular political slant. *The Conversation* (https://theconversation.com/uk) is an online magazine that specialises in publishing academic research-based articles on topical subjects for a target audience of people interested in understanding the research behind the headlines.

Both newspapers and magazines usually have a broad readership and can offer a great way to summarise your work for a large audience, pointing or linking to your academic publication for those more interested readers. For either option, conversations with editorial and publishing staff about your potential contribution will be required and their input about their target audiences will be useful. One possible downside is that, compared to other public platforms, these may have the slowest turn-around time in terms of editor decisions and publishing time.

Blogs: Blogs can provide a relatively easy and more audience-accessible way to write about your research. Most do not require subscriptions and will show up readily in keyword web searches. It is easy to insert links to your other publications or refer to previous posts. Many thematic or general-interest blogs accept guest posts, so you do not necessarily have to maintain your own blog site to use this medium.

One thing to consider is that publishing in blogs is an activity that still remains largely unrecognised as scholarly activity, although this is changing and is largely institutionally specific. It is also quite possible for one blog in a sea of internet content to be essentially lost, and therefore lack impact. Ways of making blogs more visible include linking back to your University profile (Google weights academic linked pages), promoting through social media (see Chapter 10) and mentioning it in other lay publications.

Videos and slide shares: While videos are not technically 'writing for the public', video abstracts promoting your written work or supplemental video interviews are an engaging and increasingly popular way for people to receive information. Additionally, an increasing number of videos of written word content with a few key images are being used by news outlets and social media.

Similar to this, slide share platforms allow you to publish slides directly from a talk or lecture. This can be problematic if the slides are not accompanied by some text to describe and/or elaborate the content. For both of these platforms, it is important to provide links to the original academic work and ensure no copyright is being breached.

Books or chapters: Books for general audiences can, in some instances, be published with a more relaxed process than academic books and are often looking for 'expert' voices to comment on, or summarise, an area of research. Here you may give opinions or your own expert views on a topic, influencing the readers about how to employ or apply the research. These sorts of publication may be written by a single author or a team. They will require more time and rounds of editing before final publication, although you may have more guidance and support for the writing and promotion of the material. While these will often be considered as scholarly work (depending on the content), they may not have as large an impact as open access platforms because of the associated cost.

Trade publications: We consider this broad category for anything intended to share general news, opinions or ideas among practitioners of a specific industry or field, such as trade journals, magazines, policy papers, business reports, and so on. These are narrower in audience scope, so they will not have the mass appeal as other platforms, but they can be very impactful within a specific discipline. We consider these as part of writing for a general (though more specific) audience because they are not typically peer reviewed.

With all of this choice, where should you choose to publish? The answer to this question will depend mainly on the audience you are trying to reach. It is important to think about what your audience is likely to read and be influenced by. Activity 8.2 will help you determine how and where you should publish, based on understanding your audience better.

Activity 8.2

How do lay audiences find information?

How and where do those people you regularly encounter find information? The goal of this activity is to increase your awareness of, and empathy for, how those outside your discipline (and outside academia) find information. This may take some time to compile.

You can use friends, family, undergraduate students or collaborators outside academia. Try to get answers from at least five different people, each with different backgrounds, education, professional or research experience. Ask them to spend 10–15 minutes

(Continued)

finding information about the key message you want to convey. Then ask them the following questions:

1. Where did you start to look for information on (*your topic of research here*)? What resources did you have at your disposal to use?
2. What information did you find most easily?
3. How did you read the information? Did you read from start to finish, skim, look at illustrations first, or use some other method?
4. Assuming you could not simply ask the researcher/author, what was your process if you came across a word or phrase you did not understand?
5. Do you feel you have a better understanding of the topic after this exercise?

Once you have engaged several different people in this activity, you will start to get an idea of how people find information. It is also likely that one answer came up that was not addressed in the platform list above: Wikipedia. Wiki gets a huge amount of traffic every single hour and is a common point-of-call for many people seeking information quickly. It is also easily editable and a fast way to communicate with the public about new research. This may simply entail updating a sentence or a line within a well-developed page to reflect the new contribution your research has made to the field. If there is no well-defined page on your research area, the prospect of creating a page about your research area may be an interesting potential opportunity. The downside is that this is not going to count towards your official publication record. Nevertheless, it will get your message out to people and, if you put the citation(s) of your work within the page, it will serve as a good way to promote your research (see Chapter 10).

Getting to know how those around you find information is a good place to start when considering where you might target writing for the public space. However, your ability to understand all audiences is limited. One extremely valuable resource is your institution's press office. There will be people there who will happily talk to you about your lay publication plans. For instance, they probably have contacts they can use to find a good home for your lay publication. Press office staff will also be able to help guide you on writing style for the various publications. This is of great value because the writing style for lay publication is quite different from a typical academic style.

Adjusting your writing style for the lay audience

For many of us in the academy, years have been spent learning and honing our scholastic writing skills. Therefore, we recognise that it is not a trivial task to unlearn some of those habits in order to write for general audiences. Moreover, because of your familiarity with the academic audience, you may have grown more comfortable writing for it; understanding the people and process helps you become adept at predicting where reviewers might notice the weaker or more controversial points of your work. In writing for general audiences, you may be much more uncertain about how your audience will respond. We assert, then, that mastering this skill requires courage to confront the unknown. From that first step, it will then take a commitment to practise and persevere and, importantly, it will require dedication to understanding each new audience. The guidance in the next sections will help you make a confident start.

Clear and jargon-free language

When writing for a lay audience, it is important to use language that is clear and accessible to them. The first step is to avoid jargon. Jargon words are those specialist words that have specific technical meaning, often describing a whole concept in relatively few words. Jargon does not necessarily imply complex or sophisticated language. Take, for example, the words 'model', 'qualitative' or 'significant'. These words have very different meanings across different academic disciplines. Within a speciality area, the use of jargon serves to simplify communication. All members of that community understand the specific meaning of the jargon word; therefore, no other explanation is needed. When communicating outside the speciality area, these jargon words can lead to confusion and misunderstanding.

It is important to address one of the biggest myths about communicating research to lay audiences: writing in a clear way, without jargon, is not 'dumbing-down' or demeaning your research. Just because a person does not understand, or even want to understand, your jargon words or their associated phenomena, does not mean they are not intelligent enough to understand the parts of your research that are important to them. Every field of work has its own jargon. You do not want your doctor or your mechanic to dumb anything down for you; you want them to explain the relevant information in a way that you can understand it, in order to make your own intelligent decisions. This is how your target audiences will also feel. They do not need to understand the specialist language or the background and underlying theories of your research; they have their own specialisms to focus on. What they want to understand from you is how your research is important for their lives, and they want this to be presented to them in a clear way.

That being said, eliminating jargon is often easier said than done. Because we have become so accustomed to using our jargon words and phrases, we sometimes do not even recognise we are doing so. To help, Rakedzon et al. (2017) published an online jargon identifier that researchers can use to help them make their writing more accessible (http://scienceandpublic.com/). Activity 8.3 introduces you to this freely available tool.

Activity 8.3

Identifying jargon

Locate an abstract you have written for a conference or academic publication. Take a minute to go through the abstract yourself and note any jargon words. Next, copy and paste the abstract into http://scienceandpublic.com/. Did you identify all the words that could be considered jargon? Which ones did you miss? What was your suitability for the general public score? Note: the higher, the better.

Challenge activity: Now rewrite this abstract without using these jargon words and check the score on your rewritten abstract. Were you able to make it more accessible?

When trying to avoid jargon, you may find it a struggle to come up with other words or phrases that sufficiently explain the meaning you are trying to convey. Sometimes using analogies or images can help you get your meaning across when precise words fail. It is not easy to communicate complicated research in a clear, broadly accessible manner. This is something that will take practice accompanied by informed feedback. Talking about your research with audiences you are interested in publishing for can be helpful. When having a conversation, it is easier to tell whether or not your analogy was successful. When using analogies and metaphors, be careful to consider whether the audience is as familiar with the referents as you are. For instance, in everyday English in the UK, something that is useless is described as a chocolate teapot. This is funny for some audiences but incomprehensible to those who do not make tea in pots but rely on teabags or do not drink tea at all.

The more people from different backgrounds you talk to about your research, the better you will get at identifying words and phrases that successfully convey the meaning you wish to express. In future, when your grandparent or cousin asks about your research, take the time to really explain it and ask them what they think about it. What is most interesting to them? Was there anything that they found concerning? When we only talk about our research to those who know our jargon, we never learn how to explain our work to people outside our field.

Structuring a lay publication

Words are not the only difference between academic and lay writing; the structure of the publication should also be different. Academic publications are often written in a format that is unfriendly towards the non-academic audience. This is because these publications need to provide enough details about the background to provide context and legitimise the novelty of the work, the methods used to allow for peer evaluation, and the further exploration or replication of methods. The structure of academic articles focuses on building up an argument, grounded in past research findings and theoretical underpinnings. It is common for the big picture not to be fully revealed until the Discussion/Conclusion sections.

Lay publications are written very differently. They lead with the main point in the first sentence. In a way, lay publication is structured inversely to many academic publications. This means that in lay publications the big 'so what?' question must be answered early in the publication, often in the very first sentence. Lay audiences do not have enough interest invested in your key message to struggle through thousands of words and complex arguments to get to the main point; they want it right up front, ideally in that critical first sentence.

This means that the first paragraph of a lay publication is critical. It should be dedicated to explaining specifically why your research is important to the target audience. It should contain a summary of all the important details, that is, the What, Where, When, Who and Why of the article, in a way that is tailored to the readership you are targeting. This paragraph must meet the audience on their terms, acknowledging what they know, what they understand, what their lives are like, while clearly explaining why your research is important to their world.

For lay publications, further evidence and argument are introduced after the first paragraph. However, remember that your key message for this audience is different from your key message for academics, so you will be building a very different argument. It may be that your key message is that, based on your findings, adapting professional practice would be beneficial. Therefore, your argument aimed at people in this profession would have to address how this could be achieved practically to benefit their work or their clients. This argument is likely to have to be quite short by academic standards, so all your practice in concise writing will be extremely useful.

The structure described in this section is that of a typical lay publication. That being said, you can be more creative. The National Co-ordinating Centre for Public Engagement provides a helpful guide to using narrative to communicate with the public (www.publicengagement.ac.uk/sites/default/files/publication/how_to_use_narrative_and_storytelling.pdf).

Even more innovatively, Samuel Illingworth writes poetry to communicate science (https://thepoetryofscience.scienceblog.com/author/thepoetryofscience/). This is the truly exciting aspect of writing for a lay audience. There are fewer strict rules and guidelines for this type of publication, creating opportunities for you to express yourself in unique ways. The only true limitation is your imagination and target audience's desire to read what you write. Next, we summarise our advice for writing for your chosen lay audience in Top Tips 8.1.

Top Tips 8.1

Summary of advice presented in this chapter on writing for lay audiences

1. Avoid jargon. Consider analogies, images or translating to remove jargon from your writing, and always have someone review your writing to ensure their understanding, remembering that complicated figures are jargon too.
2. Following from this first point, unless you are writing for an audience with a known expertise in the topic (that is, professionals in a specific area), assume your audience will know very little about the topic, so ensure you explain concepts or theories clearly without jargon.
3. Highlight the 'so what?' in your research and avoid focusing on the 'how?'. You might capture their attention with a brief anecdote or scene-setting for your topic, making it relevant to your reader. You can then follow this with an explanation of what it means and/or an introduction of your key concepts or theories before moving on to rest of your article.
4. Use active verbs. This engages and tells a story and is sometimes not how we write for academic publication.
5. Most universities have public engagement offices, media relations, social media teams, researcher development, writing centres, and so on. Use these early and often to find opportunities to write new pieces, receive feedback on written work and to get help with proposals for new submissions.
6. Work with editors. Have a quick pitch ready to give editors when you see a topic trending that you are interested in writing about. Ask the editors for information about their readership. Be prepared for big changes to your text and do not take offence, but ensure your important points have not been misrepresented.
7. Let your personality show when appropriate. The great opportunity in writing for general audiences is that often you are writing on your opinion or offering

commentary on a topic. In building your professional brand, this is a great opportunity to let your personality show. You can be lively, insert humour or engage your audience with story-telling or characters. Let your *voice* become a part of your brand.

8. Do not be afraid to try! We stated earlier that this process takes courage. Putting your work into the public space can be intimidating, but the benefits are worth the risk!

Throughout this part of the book, we have looked at different writing styles and genres that researchers may engage with to communicate their research to a variety of different audiences. It is through reaching out to different people in different ways that research is able to be more widely used and to have a greater benefit both to the academic community and to the wider society. The more people read about your research, the greater the chance someone will use it, creating impact. In the next part of the book, we discuss how you can help to ensure that your wonderfully written work reaches the broadest possible audience, and how you can proactively monitor and communicate the impact of your research publication.

Further reading

Badgett, L. (2015) *The Public Professor: How to Use Your Research to Change the World*. New York: New York University Press.

Brent Zook, K. (2015) Academics: leave your ivory towers and pitch your work to the media. *The Guardian*, 23 September, www.theguardian.com/higher-education-network/2015/sep/23/academics-leave-your-ivory-towers-and-pitch-your-work-to-the-media.

Kuehne, L.M. and Olden, J.D. (2015) Lay summaries needed to enhance science communication. *Proceedings of the National Academy of Science*, 112(12): 3585–3586.

Liang, X., Su, L.Y.F., Yeo, S.K., Scheufele, D.A., Brossard, D., Xenos, M., Nealey, P. and Corley, E. (2014) Building buzz: (scientists) communicating science in new media environments. *Journalism Mass Communication Quarterly*, 91(4): 772–791.

Montgomery, S.L. (2017) *Writing for General, Non-Academic Audiences: Benefits, Opportunities, Issues*. 12 September. https://jsis.washington.edu/news/writing-general-non-academic-audiences-benefits-opportunities-issues/.

O'Leary, Z. (2007) *The Social Science Jargon Buster*. London: SAGE.

Peters, H.P., Brossard, D., de Cheveigné, S., Dunwoody, S., Kallfass, M., Miller, S. and Tsuchida, S. (2008) Science communication: interactions with the mass media. *Science*, 321(5886): 204–205.

Rakedzon, T., Segev, E., Yosef, R. and Baram-Tsabari, A. (2017) Automatic jargon identifier for scientists engaging with the public and science communication educators. *PLoS One*, 12(8): e0181742.

Reeves, J., Starbuck, S. and Yeung, A. (2020) *Success in Research: Inspiring Collaboration and Engagement*. London: SAGE.

Schalet, A. (2016) Should writing for the public count toward tenure? *The Conversation*. https://theconversation.com/should-writing-for-the-public-count-toward-tenure-63983.

Wai, J. and Miller, D. (2015) Here's why academics should write for the public. *The Conversation*. https://theconversation.com/heres-why-academics-should-write-for-the-public-50874

PART III
Maximising the impact

9

How can you make your research Open Access?

Guest authors: Christine Daoutis and Montserrat Rodriguez-Marquez

In this chapter you will:

- Discover the background and key concepts of open access
- Explore ways to make your research openly available
- Discover the rewards of sharing your research openly online
- Dispel some common myths
- Explore institutions' and funders' open access requirements
- Think more broadly around open scholarship practices

Does everyone have access to scholarly research?

In Chapter 1 we discussed publication as a means to sharing our research with others, reaching both within our scholarly circles and with audiences beyond, to stimulate debate, prompt new ideas and advance knowledge. We saw that academic publications – whether journal articles, conference proceedings or monographs – are currently the most established routes to publishing: it is through these channels that our research is evaluated, improved and disseminated.

Yet, the very same channels that are meant to enable us to communicate our research are also the ones placing barriers to accessing it. The content of traditional journals is kept behind a paywall, available only to subscribers – at considerable cost. Even for subscribers who access the content, copyright restrictions usually prohibit any further sharing: typically, user rights do not extend beyond downloading and limited copying. Access to conference proceedings and monographs is similarly restricted to specific user groups. Look at Information Box 9.1 to find a few key facts about publishing trends.

Information Box 9.1

Key trends in scholarly publication

- **Growing volume of journal articles and e-books**. Over *3 million journal articles* are published annually in the Science, Technology, Engineering, Mathematics and Medical (STEMM) disciplines; this is just English-language articles. This number is increasing by about 4% per year. STEMM e-books are also on a steep rise in publication rate.
- **Oligopoly of academic publishers**. The journal publishing market is dominated by a few large commercial publishers, namely: Reed-Elsevier, Wiley-Blackwell, Taylor & Francis, Springer and Sage. This is reflected in a high concentration of publications in journals owned by those publishers, a trend seen mainly in the Social Sciences but also in STEMM. Publications in the Humanities are more evenly distributed.
- **High journal subscription costs**. Journal subscriptions globally cost academic libraries billions every year. While it is hard to estimate exact costs per country, some data have begun to emerge. In the UK, the estimate is an average spend of about £80 million per year on the top five publishers alone. To provide the widest possible access to their researchers, libraries buy journal subscriptions in bundles. This model is known as the 'Big Deal'. While these deals may appear to reduce costs, their pricing is not transparent and they reduce flexibility, forcing libraries to buy journals included within the package that they do not need.
- **Challenges for monographs**. The volume of books and monographs published in the Social Sciences and Humanities (SSH) is hard to estimate, due to the lack of transparency/availability of relevant data. Monographs remain a very recognised publication channel in many disciplines, but they are expensive both to produce and to buy. The general trend is that libraries have to cut their book budgets to meet the costs of journal subscriptions.
- **Permission barriers**. A typical paper published in a **subscription journal** carries a copyright notice prohibiting most uses of the work other than downloading or copying it for personal use. Traditionally, authors have allowed this by signing away their rights to the publisher. As a result, even the people who read this research are very limited in how they can share it further and build on it.

This information highlights what is known as the 'crisis in scholarly communication': access to scholarly literature is increasingly unaffordable for everyone. Academic and research institutions – including wealthier institutions, such as Harvard – are struggling to provide access to the scholarly literature their staff and students need. This includes articles and books written by staff they themselves employ or fund. At the same time, commercial publishers, especially those dominating the market, have profit margins of 35–40%.

Crucially, the access problem affects us not only as readers, but also as authors. We seldom get paid for our publications; we publish for education and impact. We want others to find, download, read, cite and build upon our research. Unfortunately, this is something that only journal subscribers can do, and still only within limits.

Before we consider how some barriers to access can be lifted, engage with Activity 9.1 to see how the access problem affects you.

Activity 9.1

Barriers to access, barriers to impact

Think of three papers that you recently read. Log out of your institution's account and look up these papers. If you were not affiliated to a subscribing institution, how much would it cost you to read them?

Write down at least three audiences you think should have access to your research; for example, practitioners, policy makers or the general public. How would they benefit from reading your publications and what do you think are the implications – for you and for them – if they do not have access?

Lifting barriers to access

What do you do when you do not have access to a journal article? In the pre-online era, you would probably have asked your library to order a copy, or you would have contacted the author directly. Most of the time the author would have been happy to send you a published off-print, a newly-accepted manuscript or even, in many cases, a pre-reviewed version.

The internet opened new possibilities in how research is communicated and shared. What was before an informal, sporadic exchange between researchers – for example, emailing copies of early manuscripts – could now become centralised and systematic, allowing discoverability and immediate access. This is indeed what happened: as early as 1991, the American physicist Paul Ginsparg founded what is now known as ArXiv (pronounced archive), an electronic archive of scientific papers, to facilitate the storage and sharing of early, pre-refereed manuscripts (pre-prints). What is now referred to as an e-print server was born.

ArXiv is the first example of a scientist-led initiative, primarily focused on pre-refereed papers, made possible by the internet. It would take over another decade to formulate a collective call for access to peer-reviewed scholarly literature:

> An old tradition and a new technology have converged to make possible an unprecedented public good. The old tradition is the willingness of scientists and scholars to publish the fruits of their research in scholarly journals without payment, for the sake of inquiry and knowledge. The new technology is the internet. The public good they make possible is the world-wide electronic distribution of the peer-reviewed journal literature and completely free and unrestricted access to it by all scientists, scholars, teachers, students, and other curious minds. Removing access barriers to this literature will accelerate research, enrich education, share the learning of the rich with the poor and the poor with the rich, make this literature as useful as it can be, and lay the foundation for uniting humanity in a common intellectual conversation and quest for knowledge. (The Budapest Open Access Initiative, 2002)

The declaration goes on to define free access to literature and indicate the means for achieving it. Before we go on to visit these definitions in more detail, it is worth reflecting, using Reflection Point 9.1, on the wider context in which scholarly knowledge is viewed.

Reflection Point 9.1

Lifting barriers to access

To what extent do you think that the 'free distribution of peer-reviewed journal literature' lifts barriers to access? What about other types of publications?

'Removing barriers to literature will lay the foundation for uniting humanity in a common intellectual conversation.' Can you think of any other barriers, besides paywalls, which need to be lifted for research to be free for all?

Open access: overview, benefits and concerns

Definitions

Open access (OA) ensures that scholarly literature is freely available online to anyone with access to the internet. More specifically, open access literature is:

- **Free of charge**. Users can access the full text, not just the abstract or bibliographic details, without paying any fees.
- **Free to re-use**. Merely removing price barriers is not adequate for open access; at least some permission restrictions should be lifted as well, enabling readers to

build upon the work. Open access papers vary in relation to how many copyright/ permissions restrictions have been removed. For example, many 'open access' papers are free to download and read, but not free to adapt or use in a commercial context. The broadest definition of open access (as formulated, for example, in the Budapest Open Access declaration) is one where all financial, technical and legal barriers have been removed, allowing maximum re-use of the research as long as the author is properly acknowledged.

- **Scholarly**. Open access may include any scholarly literature, both published and unpublished: for example, journal articles, conference proceedings, theses, book chapters, monographs, working papers, reports, teaching resources and textbooks, software, images, data and arts research outputs like compositions, performances, sound recordings and artworks. These can be born digital or digitised retrospectively. As we will see, the main focus in the last two decades has been primarily on freeing peer-reviewed papers published in journals and conference proceedings and providing open access to doctoral theses. Initiatives to free access to monographs are also emerging. In this chapter we focus mainly on journal articles, monographs and theses.
- **Immediate**. Access to this literature should not be delayed. As we will see later, the timing of open access is still one of the biggest barriers in providing access; it is mainly imposed by publishers, but often by the authors too.

Types of open access

The first thing that comes to mind when 'open access' is mentioned is open access publishing. Most researchers we speak to also assume that, in this case, payment of a fee to the publisher is necessary. This is not true. Open access publishing is just one option; it often requires a publication fee, but this is not always the case. This route is known as **Gold open access**.

The other option involves you sharing your paper online. Essentially, you publish in a traditional journal but keep the right to share your work online as well. More and more publishers allow you to do this under certain conditions. The published version still sits behind a paywall, but you make available your own version. Usually you can share the accepted peer-reviewed manuscript. In this way, non-subscribers can still find and read your work. This option is called author self-archiving or **Green open access**.

While these routes refer mainly to journal articles and conference proceedings, similar models apply to books. We will explain in detail how you can practise these options later on in this chapter.

Based on your understanding of open access so far, engage with Activity 9.2.

Benefits and concerns

Think of a piece of research you are currently writing up or planning to write up. This can be your doctoral thesis, a journal article, a book chapter or any other scholarly work.

Looking at the definitions of open access, how do you feel about sharing your work in this way? Can you see the benefits of making your work freely accessible? Do you have any concerns? *With your own research in mind*, make a list of possible pros and cons. You will need this in the next two sections.

Benefits of open access

Making a piece of research easily discoverable and freely available on the web can open exciting opportunities, both on a small scale – say, a paper that provided the spark for your PhD proposal, a popular thesis that turned into an influential book, a conference proceeding that led to a new collaboration – and on a larger scale: the wider the adoption of open access, the easier it becomes to demonstrate its value.

The large-scale benefits have been well documented. Numerous studies have compared the citation rates of open access versus pay-walled articles. Most of those studies report a citation advantage for the open access articles; this has been demonstrated in a range of disciplines. Although citation analysis research should be interpreted with caution, overall the evidence seems to support that, when other factors have been taken into account (for example, timing of publication, selection bias, and so on), freely available literature gets more downloads and citations than restricted research. As citation impact features highly in league tables, this has obvious benefits for the authors and their institutions. The Voice of Experience 9.1 expresses this in a researcher's own words.

The rewards of open access

Engineers are trained to come up with solutions to health or societal challenges. As an academic who is also a biomedical engineer by background, I find myself leaning towards translational research; in other words, research that will translate into tools that can be used in the clinic.

Making my work open access has increased my own researcher visibility and impact within the discipline. Importantly, it has also allowed me to cross the disciplinary boundaries of biomechanics (my field), enabling me to make my research available to the clinical and biomechanical communities and, by doing so, facilitate the use of methods and models developed in-house by clinicians.

As in many other research areas, advancements and breakthroughs in my field depend on the availability of not only publications, but also research data and analysis protocols. If scientific knowledge and data are not shared, you can end up with excellent models and data that are not used by the main research beneficiaries. My current research has been planned with this in mind.

Dr Aliah Shaheen, Senior Lecturer in Biomechanics,
https://orcid.org/0000-0003-2492-8818

The benefits of open access reach beyond academic researchers. Two sources demonstrate this well. The website whoneedsaccess.org, a site dedicated to advocating public access to scientific research, presents numerous compelling cases where access to research has transformed people's lives. Harvard University's open access repository (see https://dash.harvard.edu/stories) also gathers the stories of users from around the world who accessed Harvard research. Each story recounted illustrates the huge potential of open access to lead to the innovative and the unexpected. Nowhere is this more remarkable than in biomedical research, access to which is crucial, not just to researchers, but also to the patients and their families, medical practitioners and carers. We provide examples in Activity 9.3.

Activity 9.3

How does open access improve the world?

Visit Harvard University's website https://dash.harvard.edu/stories and have a look at a few stories from different readers (you can browse them by country). Did anything strike you in these stories? How do these stories, and what you read above, compare to your notes from the previous activity?

Talk to someone outside academia about access to research. Do they have a story where access to scholarly research on the web helped them to solve a problem or discover something new? Or do they have stories about how that could have helped had they known about it?

Common concerns

Objections to open access are numerous, and are raised by publishers, institutions and the authors themselves. In many cases, these stem from a misunderstanding of what open access is intended to do; in other cases, they raise some valid questions that need to be addressed. Only in very few cases, however, are these concerns a reason for permanently restricting access. We also see an appetite by researchers for delaying online access, especially in the case of doctoral theses; this is sometimes justified and sometimes reflects a vague apprehension about sharing. Activity 9.4 discusses the most commonly expressed concerns.

Activity 9.4

Common concerns regarding open access

Consult the table 'Concerns about open access to publications and responses to them' in Appendix A, which addresses some frequently voiced worries and responses about open access. Have a look to see what is relevant to you, and compare to your own notes from Activity 9.2. Are your own concerns addressed in the table? Have the responses satisfied them?

Making open access happen: guide with best practice

It is perhaps surprising that, while in theory 'open access' is a simple and liberating idea, in practice it is implemented in a remarkably prescriptive way. There are several reasons for this, the most important of which is the control publishers historically have had, and continue to have, over the copyrights and the overall progress of open access: detailed rules about where, when and how you can share your work are written into your publishers' copyright agreements and policies. Another reason is that research institutions and funders also have a stake, and a say, in how funded research is shared and best preserved. How open access is achieved depends on the type of literature (for example, journal article, monograph, thesis) that is shared.

Journal articles

As mentioned earlier, when it comes to published journal articles and conference proceedings, there are two main routes to open access: open access publishing (Gold open access) and author self-archiving (Green open access). These options may also apply to some book chapters. As illustrated in the table in Appendix B, which summarises the key features of the two approaches, there are several differences between the two. A few points are worth highlighting here.

Publishing in a purely **open access journal** is a no-brainer, if your choice of journal is well informed – the journal's scope, editorial processes and reputation make it the most appropriate publication venue for your journal article – and your funder/institution can cover any publication costs. Note that many open access journals have a bad reputation for being low quality or using predatory practices to attract authors. While many of us associate open access with bad editorial practices, the two are separate: open access does not equal low quality.

Things become more complicated if a **subscription journal** offers a paid open access option ('**hybrid journal**'). Once your paper is accepted, the publisher will usually ask if you want to sign the standard copyright agreement or pay to make the paper open access. Before you decide to go for the paid option, consider what the standard route offers: is there also a Green option, and what sharing rights do you keep under that option? The decision you make will vary from case to case and will depend on many factors, including embargo length. Note that, while many journals only allow you to share your paper online after 6–12 (STM) or 18–24 (SSH) months, others do not impose an embargo. In those cases, the only difference between the Gold and the Green options lies in the version you are allowed to share.

Most publishers' Green policies only allow you to share your own version; not the published PDF or the proof copy. What you can usually share is the accepted manuscript, peer-reviewed and formally accepted for publication, after final corrections have been made. You may see publishers' policies referring to this version as the 'author's accepted manuscript' (AAM), 'post-print' or simply 'author's version' (typically the submitted, not reviewed version is called a 'pre-print'). As this version is peer-reviewed and does not compromise the quality of the research, sharing it is widely supported by universities and funders alike. In fact, this version is your passport to sharing your research with others. It is good practice to add it to your university's repository as soon as it is accepted, whether it stays under embargo or not.

Bearing in mind that many subscription journals will try to push the Gold option, it is important that you are well informed before you make a decision. Activity 9.5 will further your understanding of these options.

Activity 9.5

Gold or Green open access?

Think of a journal you have published in or plan to publish in. Look up the journal's policy – usually under Instructions for Authors – or look the journal up in http://sherpa.ac.uk/romeo/

(Continued)

Does the journal support open access? What options does it offer?

Based on the information we discussed, when would you choose the Green option and when would you choose the Gold option?

Tip: Consider how long the embargo is, which option allows you to meet any funder requirements, and whether there are funds to cover publication costs. Does the Green option let you reach your audiences without paying for open access?

Monographs

While it is true that the open access movement has focused heavily on journal articles, in the last few years we have seen activity in opening access to monographs as well. In fact, the pace of change is faster for monographs than for journal articles, with various innovative models being tried globally. This is important, as the monograph (see Chapter 7) has a central place in the Arts and Humanities in particular, while also being important in the Social Sciences and some STEMM areas.

Various studies suggest that open access monographs are widely used, both by academic and non-academic audiences and across a wide range of countries. Not surprisingly, for example, online discovery and usage of Google Books has increased for open access titles. Like other types of research, open access monographs dramatically increase the potential for their content to be used in research and scholarship as well as in teaching, with most restrictions removed.

This is not to say that the transition to digital open access monographs is without its challenges. There are several cultural, copyright and financial issues to consider: emerging publishing models address these challenges in different ways. If you intend to publish a monograph, it is worth considering what options you may have and how they would best fit your research area and the audiences you want to reach. We outline some of these in Information Box 9.2.

Information Box 9.2

Publishing your monograph open access

If you plan to publish a monograph, the following options are worth exploring. The publishers and initiatives listed below use various business models, from a classic 'pay-to-publish' model to crowdsourcing/consortia-funded models and from commercial publishers to not-for-profit, community-run initiatives.

- **Commercial publishers**, including Palgrave, Springer and Brill, offer an open access option alongside a traditional model. Prices may vary by book size and range from £6,000 to £12,000.
- **University presses** may offer more affordable options, as they are often subsidised. From the more established Cambridge University Press and University of California Press to relatively new presses like UCL Press in the UK and Athabasca University Press in Canada, various models are offered to support monographs. Check if your university has, or is affiliated to, an open press: as a publishing member of staff or student, you may pay less or not at all.
- **Open access presses** specialising in monographs include Open Book Publishers, Open Humanities Press and the French initiative Open Edition. Some of these operate a '**freemium**' model: the digital version is published open access with enhanced digital versions or print-on-demand options available as well, to subsidise production costs.

It is clear that we have a long way to go as far as open monographs are concerned; however, in terms of innovation and willingness to place transparency and openness above financial profit, monographs already lead the way, ahead of journal publishing. It is worth exploring these developments further within your discipline and possibly discover links to other disciplines. Open Humanities Press, in particular, goes well beyond simply publishing monographs; it is a great starting point if you want to engage further with open initiatives.

Theses

The benefits to open theses are the same as with any other piece of research: widest possible visibility, usage and impact. In the case of theses, the benefits may be even more dramatic: while journal articles, for example, are available only to the lucky ones who subscribe to the content, theses are, paradoxically, virtually unavailable to everyone, even though by definition they are already in the public domain. A hard copy of the thesis sitting on the shelf in a library is as good as restricted: very few even know it exists, let alone can have immediate access to it. Electronic thesis databases are changing this, and open access to their full content widens the potential for innovation – and prevents others from repeating the same research – in ways not imagined before.

Compared to the challenges and options related to open access journal articles and monographs, open theses seem straightforward. Unlike commercial publications, when it comes to theses there are, in most cases, no conflicting financial interests, major rights conflicts or any other obstacles preventing you from sharing your thesis online. Yet, we still see cases where authors and their supervisors are reluctant to share a thesis before its content is published. Earlier on in this chapter we addressed the most common concerns around sharing theses. We saw that, while it is important to address issues of confidentiality, in many cases we can overcome our reservations and share the work online, as indeed most universities now require.

Preparing and sharing your thesis for open access is simple, but may require some planning. Look at Top Tips 9.1.

Top Tips 9.1

Making your thesis open access

1. **Know your university's policy**. Most universities will expect you to put the final version of your thesis in the university's open access repository. This is the 'version of record', as approved by the examiners after any corrections. It is worth knowing what is required of you early on, to avoid any last-minute surprises at the very end.
2. **Clear copyright as you go along**. To use any substantial copyrighted content not created or owned by you, you will need to get written permission from the copyright holder and keep any correspondence on file. This may take a while, so it is good practice to clear permissions as you go along. If in doubt, talk to the copyright adviser at your university. Always acknowledge the creator of the work you are using, even if you have permission.
3. **Deal with any commercial/sensitive/confidential material early on**. If you need to restrict access to part, or all, of your thesis, you should plan ahead. Talk to your supervisor and/or your university's Intellectual Property (IP) office and always deal with any paperwork in good time.
4. **Write for openness, not just for the examiners**. Your thesis is the product of a long learning process: you need to demonstrate to the examiners your depth of understanding of your topic. However, a thesis is not just a piece of coursework; it does make an original contribution to your field. Write it with this in mind: others will find it, read it and build on it.
5. **Do not be scared to share it**. This is probably one of the first public contributions you make in your field. It should be complementary, not identical to, any publications you get out of the same research. Enjoy sharing it with the world!

Bringing it all together: making the most of open access

So far, we have reviewed the options available to you for making your publications and thesis open access. Here, in Top Tips 9.2, we give some further advice to help you make the most of open access.

Top Tips 9.2

Make the most of open access

Ensure that the research you share online is:

1. **Accurately attributed to you**. Get an **ORCID iD**, if you do not already have one. An ORCID iD is a unique digital identifier (a string of numbers, in other words) permanently and unequivocally linked to your name. If your name is the same or similar to other researchers', publications may not be attributed accurately to you. ORCID prevents this: you claim authorship by linking all your publications to this identifier. Similarly, if you have published under different names or variants of your name, or if you change affiliations, your ORCID identifier ensures continuity. ORCID is already adopted by many institutions, funders and publishers. To register or update your profile visit https://support.orcid.org/.

2. **Easily identifiable and discoverable**. Like your name, your publication itself should be unambiguously identified, so that others can discover and cite it accurately. Publishers assign a unique identifier (DOI: digital object identifier) to most journal articles and some conference proceedings and book chapters. A DOI also provides a permanent link to the record. If the research you share online has not been assigned a DOI by a publisher – for example, if it is a thesis, a dataset or an unpublished report – speak to the library in your institution about getting one. Many universities have now adopted DOIs for all their doctoral theses.

    When you share your publication record online, it is important that you include the DOI as well as other information (metadata) that will make the publication more discoverable: an accurate title, an abstract and keywords and the correct author names, as well as the DOI, plus any other bibliographic details will ensure this.

3. **Shared under a licence allowing the widest possible re-use**. Creative Commons Licences (CC-licences) are open copyright licences specifying how others can re-use someone's work. If a publication is shared under a Creative Commons Licence, you will usually see one of the six images below displayed next to it:

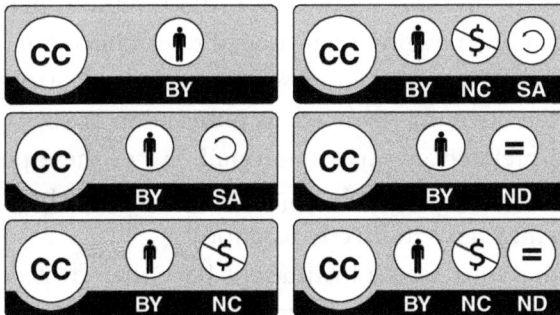

Figure 9.1   Creative Commons Licence

(Continued)

Each type of CC-licence tells readers how they can re-use the work. For example, the NC sign means non-commercial (any commercial re-use is not allowed), ND means non-derivative (the work can be shared but not adapted) and SA means Share-Alike (people re-sharing the work must do so under the same licence terms). For all types of licence, the creator must always be fully credited and any other requirements the creator specifies, for example linking to their website, must be met.

Most publications published open access are shared under the most liberal of the licences (CC-BY), which allows maximum re-use. Which licence you choose will depend on how you want others to re-use your work. As we will see, funders may also require, or recommend, a specific licence.

For more information on Creative Commons Licences see https://creativecommons.org/share-your-work/licensing-types-examples/.

4. **Further publicised to key audiences**. Open access is only the starting point for research communication. Once your paper is online, you should make sure that your key audiences are alerted to it and know they can access it. You can, at the very least, tweet about it or link to it from any academic social networking sites on which you are active. Sites like **ResearchGate** and academia.edu are a great way of connecting with your colleagues and showcasing your research; but, to avoid copyright breaches, just make sure that the actual paper is always hosted in your university's or funder's repository. Chapters 2, 8 and 10 suggest further ways in which you can promote and communicate your research to various audiences.

Open access policies

Once an initiative launched by researchers, open access is now being embraced globally by governments, research funders and institutions. For example, over 80 national funders from various European countries, Argentina, Australia, Brazil, Canada, India, Japan, Mexico, South Africa, the US and others have published policies requiring or encouraging their funded researchers to make their publications open on the web. Charities and research institutions strongly support open access as well, often covering open access publication costs. While approaches, requirements and preferences vary, the overall aim of these policies is to make scholarly literature widely available, especially to those who cannot otherwise access it, but who may have indirectly paid for it.

Universities and other research institutions have their own policies, which are usually aligned to national requirements. In the UK, for example, open access to journal articles and conference proceedings is already a requirement in universities' research assessment, and it is anticipated that open monographs will follow suit in a few years. These mandates have made senior managers and researchers take notice, if they had not already: the percentage of open access publication is on the rise as a result.

In September 2018, cOAlition S, an international consortium of research funders led by Science Europe, launched a new open access initiative called Plan S. Built around 10 general principles, the initiative aims to accelerate and transform scholarly communication by not only requiring open access to publications, but also, more crucially, pushing towards the development of efficient, sustainable and transparent publishing models. The initiative is being supported internationally by a number of national funders and charities. It is anticipated that, in the next few years, many institutions will align their policies and practices to Plan S.

Whatever your thoughts about open access are, it is essential that you understand any policies and requirements your university and/or funder has in place regarding open access to research. Activity 9.6 will help you to be up to date with current requirements.

Activity 9.6

Open access requirements

Thinking of your university and any organisation funding your research, including your doctoral thesis, look up their policies on sharing research outputs. Print out the policy and note the key points.

Use the table below to make sure you understand and meet the requirements.

	University/Research organisation	Funder 1	Funder 2
Requires open access			
Type of output			
Where to share			
When to share by			
Options supported (Gold, Green)			
Where to share			
Licence specified?			
Funds available?			
Notes			

Beyond open access: towards a culture of openness

Throughout this chapter we have discussed the current context and trends related to sharing your publications openly online. Where appropriate, we have given you information, advice and quick tips that are especially useful when navigating publishers', funders' and institutions' expectations and choices. By now you should be aware of what open access means, in practical terms, in your own discipline, and what you should/can do to support it.

At the same time, 'openness' in research is more than just complying with policies or knowing how to choose a publishing option, both of which, of course, are essential to your professional development and to applying best practice. 'Openness' is, in fact, more than open access to literature. Initiatives like 'open research', 'open science', 'open knowledge' or 'open scholarship' look beyond freeing access to publications, to support a culture where researchers work transparently and collaboratively to share, not just publications, but also ideas, research designs, research findings, resources and software, and feedback (open peer review). There is a plethora of open initiatives out there for you to explore and engage with. The one that is rapidly taking shape is **open research** data as you can see in Voice of Experience 9.2.

Voice of Experience 9.2

Open data

What if, after reading an interesting publication, you could immediately download the data to verify the findings or reuse in your own project? Well, increasingly you can! Publications often include a statement outlining where and how you can access the data that underpin them. Underlying this movement is a recognition of high-quality, reusable data as a important outputs on a par with publications. Many universities, funders, journals and scholarly professional organisations have endorsed open data policies as a central tenet of academic integrity, recognising it as a way to advance scholarship faster, facilitate transparency and promote reproducibility. While some disciplines have long had strong cultures of sharing data (for example, astronomy and genomics), data-sharing practices are now being embraced across all types of scholarship.

Of course, there are some good reasons why data cannot, or should not, be shared (for instance, ethical, legal and commercial considerations), but a common misconception is that sharing data is an open/closed binary. There exist myriad ways to share data in controlled environments and to vet potential reusers! This includes restricting access to the data, asking users to sign non-disclosure agreements and seeking out specialist data repositories to handle really sensitive data.

How can you make your data more open? Well, you can ask yourself: is your data FAIR? FORCE11 (10.1038/sdata.2016.18) proposed the FAIR principles in 2016 to promote better data sharing. FAIR stands for Findable, Accessible, Interoperable and Reusable. Does your data meet these criteria?

Findable – How do people know your data exist? Is there a data access statement and DOI linking to the data in your publication or output?

Accessible – How can people get the data? Are the data freely downloadable from a data repository?

Interoperable – Are there technological barriers to using your data? Are the code or scripts included? Are there standards within your discipline you can adopt to make the data easier to use?

Reuseable – Is there enough documentation to understand the data? Did you apply a licence so people know how they can use your data (for instance, for non-commercial purposes only)?

The key to making data-sharing easy is coming up with a plan before you even start your project for how you will hit these criteria. Then, once your data are FAIR, you will not only be demonstrating your academic integrity with easily verifiable and reusable data, but you'll benefit from increased citations (10.7717/peerj.175) and potential new collaborations!

Dr Alice Motes, Research Data and Preservation Manager,
https://orcid.org/0000-0001-6638-9213

Managing and sharing research data is the next step to complement the open sharing of publications, but, as mentioned, we expect to see even more. The last activity of this chapter, Activity 9.7, involves your making both a practical action plan and reflecting on how you can further explore and engage with activities aimed at more open, transparent and collaborative research.

Activity 9.7

Your open research plan

Using the table below, choose the areas that you feel you need to explore further. Use these to build an action plan.

Open access is often described as 'radical', but it really is just about reaching out to share what belongs to everyone anyway. Consider engaging with innovative models of sharing and communicating research. Pick one area relevant to your research (for example, open review models, disruptive media, open educational resources, public engagement) and look up the latest developments, and how you can contribute to it.

(Continued)

	Next step	Notes
The basics		
• Share my publications/ thesis/data/other outputs in a repository		
• Understand my publisher's copyright agreement and how it affects my research		
• Understand Creative Commons Licences and how they affect my research		
• Consider making my monograph open access		
• Seek advice and support before I decide to pay for open access publishing		
• Understand and meet my funders' and university's requirements regarding publications and data		
Beyond the basics...		
• Engage with at least one aspect of open research in my own team. Encourage debate with my colleagues and students/champion initiatives I feel strongly about		

Having created your action plan for open engagement, the next chapters will focus on how to further promote your research and encourage a wide range of people to use it.

Further reading

Budapest Open Access Initiative. Available at: www. budapestopenaccessinitiative.org/read
cOAlition S (2018) *Plan S: Making Full and Immediate Open Access a Reality.* Available at: www.coalition-s.org/
Collins, E., Milloy, C. and Stone, G. (2015) Guide to Open Access Monograph Publishing for Arts, Humanities and Social Science Researchers: Helping

Researchers to Understand the Opportunities and Challenges of Publishing a Scholarly Monograph in Open Access. Available at: http://openaccess.city.ac.uk/12373/1/Guide-to-open-access-monograph-publishing-for-researchers-final.pdf

Piwowar, H.A. and Vision, T.J. (2013) Data reuse and the open data citation advantage. *PeerJ*, 1: e175, https://doi.org/10.7717/peerj.175

Neylon, C. (2015) The limits on 'open': why knowledge is not a public good and what to do about it. *Science in the Open* (Blog). http://cameronneylon.net/blog/the-limits-on-open-why-knowledge-is-not-a-public-good-and-what-to-do-about-it/

Tennant, J.P., Crane, H., Crick, T., Davila, J., Enkhbayar, A., Havemann, J., Kramer, B., Martin, R., Masuzzo, P., Nobes, A., Rice, C., Rivera-López, B., Ross-Hellauer, T., Sattler, S., Thacker, P.D. and Vanholsbeeck, M. (2019) Ten hot topics around scholarly publishing. *Publications*, 7: 34.

Tennant, J.P., Waldner, F., Damien, C., Jacques, D.C., Masuzzo, P., Collister, L.B. and Hartgerink, S.H.J. (2016) *The Academic, Economic and Societal Impacts of Open Access: An Evidence-Based Review*. [version 3; peer review: 4 approved, 1 approved with reservations]. *F1000 Research*, 5(632). https://doi.org/10.12688/f1000research.8460.3

10

What can you do to promote your publications?

In this chapter you will:

- Learn how to integrate promotion into the entire publication journey from planning to post-publication
- Create a promotion plan that parallels your overall publication plan
- Understand how to utilise conventional avenues for publication promotion successfully
- Explore new methods of promotion to expand your ability to promote your work to an ever-broader audience
- Think about how to be flexible in your promotion approaches so that you can adapt easily to new ways of engaging others with your research

Whether your publication reaches and influences your intended audience is much more than luck. In this chapter, we will look at ways to ensure your publication is seen, read and used by as many people as possible. Promoting your publications is not something that is done once the paper or book or chapter, and so on, is in print, but is an ongoing consideration throughout the course of your publication journey. Before your work is published, there are various activities you can engage in to ensure that it gets noticed. This starts with your initial publication strategy, as discussed in Chapter 1, and should be considered as part of your plan for each individual publication, as discussed in Chapter 4.

Preparing to publish articles

With estimates of over 2 million journal articles published each year (Eveleth, 2014; AJE, 2016), you may want to consider how to get your article to stand out from the crowd. In Chapter 4 we discuss how to decide where to publish your work. This will depend on several factors, but if getting your article read, cited and used by your intended audience is a priority for you, one factor to consider is where (what journals) the most citations in your field are occurring. In other words, where is your intended audience already looking for your type of work? You may also want to consider how accessible your selected journals are. As discussed in Chapter 9, journals that are full-text, open access and indexed by ISI are the most accessible to the widest possible audience. There is not a one-size-fits-all solution to this balance between accessibility and specific audience choices, but it is one you should consider carefully even before you begin writing, because this will determine *how* you write your article.

As you prepare your manuscript, in addition to taking the advice furnished in Chapter 5, you should look at other articles in your field that are receiving attention. Note the content, keywords or phrases, the overall tone and style of the articles, as well as the sources other researchers are citing and how they are using the citation. In this way you can weave your paper into the overall narrative of your broad research area, expanding your appeal to the widest audience. Include as many relevant references within your field as you are allowed as there is a strong relationship between the number of references a paper has and the citations that paper receives (Corbyn, 2010). Your title should be clear, descriptive and include the most relevant of the keywords or phrases you have noted in these other works. A number of these keywords should also be used in your abstract. Repeating prevalent keywords will increase the likelihood that your publication will be nearer the top of a search list, making it more likely to be read.

In preparing your article for publication, these keywords and clear messaging should run throughout your text, as well as in figures or information boxes. Often, figures will appear during web searches under 'images' and can be another avenue of attracting attention. In addition to keywords, your figure captions should have enough information to attract a reader to read your entire article. Figures themselves can also be a cite-worthy source for other researchers, especially in reviews, doctoral dissertations, presentations or infographics.

Your abstract is a crucial component for attracting attention to your article and getting it cited. It should have a clear message, including the major takeaway points from your article. Before submitting an article, get feedback on your abstract from others to ensure its clarity. Consider asking peers outside your discipline or even someone in your institution's media relations team to read through your abstract and relate what they thought its key message was. A well-written abstract, with a clear message that is accessible to a wide audience will increase your readership.

As well as being crucial in your title and abstract, keywords must be provided when submitting your article. Use as many key words as the journal allows. If you have difficulty thinking of them, use Activity 10.1 to help you generate a comprehensive list of keywords.

Activity 10.1

Determining keywords

Through this exercise you should be able to develop an extensive list of keywords to include with your publications. The aim is to extend your original list by at least 10 additional keywords.

1. Go back to the 'frequently cited' articles you identified above. Check their keywords and see if they have any you have not listed and, if applicable, include those in your list.
2. Next, consider what other terms your potential readers might be searching. Do a little investigation into the researchers citing the work you used in Step 1. Most online journals have easy ways to look up 'cited by' or 'other readers also read', making it relatively simple for you to quickly link to the articles related to this original paper. Find keywords from those articles that are relevant to your work and add them to your list.
3. If you still need a few more keywords or phrases, try a simple web search with a few of the words you already have on your list, noting titles of articles that appear in this search. From these titles you should be able to get a few more words or phrases to add to your list.

The most common ways for people to search for references is through keyword and author searches. If you have published already, it is helpful to use the same form of your name, so that all your articles appear within the same author search. For example, if you have used your middle initial in a previous publication, keep using it. Ensure any collaborators' details are also consistent with how they normally publish, because it will not be just your name people search for. If you have had a name change, you have already published with inconsistency in your name, or you have a common name, an ORCID ID may be especially important to ensure your full publication history is identified to people searching (see Chapter 9).

Preparing to publish a book

Much of the advice we listed above for articles will also follow for book or monograph publications. Keywords, a good title, a clear summary/abstract are all crucial, as is an easily searchable author name, in helping your book stand out from the crowd. The two main differences when promoting a book are the time-scale from acceptance to publishing and the support of the publishing house in promotion. The marketing team will certainly advise you on a title that will attract readers.

It may surprise you to know how important your own promotion of your book can be, despite having a publishing house supporting the project. Given the time it takes to publish a book product, there is ample opportunity for you to conduct targeted publicity for your book prior to its publication. Assuming the writing process of your book will take about a year, you will have some time to present pieces of your book at key conferences or seminars (which we discuss in the next section). You may even consider publishing articles from material you are developing within your book; these you will be able to cite in your book.

Book publications also afford a few more possibilities you may want to consider as you approach publication, for example, book festivals and prizes. Before publishing you should note key dates and requirements so that you are ready once your work is published. You should also contact your university's **media relations** or **press office** to learn about their process. They can often assist you with writing up a media-friendly summary and drawing attention for pre-orders. They often plan well in advance, so waiting to tell them once you have published may mean you miss a crucial advertising window. In Voice of Experience 10.1, an early career researcher gives three lessons learned from working with his institution's press office.

Voice of Experience 10.1

Working with the press office

1. Be very careful what goes in the press release; the release gets reported almost verbatim by other reporters.
2. Work out where you can get the funder and project names in and target them for your best efforts. As much as you try to shoehorn in your project and funder, most of the time it will not get picked up. Some of the articles are short and readers frankly do not care who funded the work. They are more interested in what has been revealed. I tried three times to put in EPSRC and CLEVER when approached for questions, but they never made it to the final article.
3. Always go to media relations when you have something published. Correction: before you have something published. They can decide if it is worth pursuing further and will offer loads of help getting it out there.

To read James' full blog post, visit: https://highimpactlowimpact.wordpress.com/2015/07/02/spreading-the-word/

Dr James Suckling, Environmental Sustainability Research Fellow

As well as your press office, you should also contact your library early, because they will often purchase copies of faculty books and can circulate them among their networks. This will ensure they get their copies on time so that they can help you to promote it. Always work with your publisher, so you are both supporting each other in the promotion of your book.

Top Tips 10.1 provides a list of actions you can take to start promoting your publication, journal article, monograph or book, even before it is in print.

Top Tips 10.1

Ten tips for promotion before publication

1. Select keywords carefully and thoroughly.
2. Use keywords and phrases in titles and abstracts or summaries.
3. Look where the most citations in your field are occurring.
4. Weave your work into the narrative of your field.
5. Keep consistent naming and affiliation for all authors (and check final prints).
6. Contact your press office early.
7. Leverage the review process for new connections.
8. Promote your work before it is published.
9. Work closely with your publisher to support each other's promotion efforts.
10. Talk about your writing and your upcoming book, virtually and face to face.

Bonus tip: Consider a video abstract for your article or book.

Video abstracts are becoming a more popular way of adding supplementary material to your article. It is a brief description of your paper in which you can use animation, demonstration and dialogue to explain your textual article further. The main purpose is to promote your paper by capturing your audience's attention and encouraging them to read your paper. Using this medium for your publication may be worth discussing with your editor or publisher. For more information on video abstracts, you might like to visit this helpful resource: http://thescientistvideographer.com/wordpress/how-to-make-a-video-abstract-for-your-next-journal-article/

After publishing

Once your publication is in print or available virtually, besides partaking in a well-earned celebration, it is time to think about the next wave of promotion activity. To do so, it is important to consider again what you wish to achieve from this publication. In Chapter 1 we suggested identifying success measures, one of which, no doubt, is getting your work into print. Hopefully, though, that is not the only measure identified. The next steps you can take to ensure your article is seen by more people, requiring minimal effort from you, are listed in Top Tips 10.2.

Top Tips 10.2

Quick ways to start promoting your publication

1. **Update your information**. Make sure your institutional and departmental websites are updated to include your new publication, with a link to the full text. If you are using Researcher IDs, check that those are also updated with the new publication. This is often set up at the submission stage, but now is the time to ensure it has gone through correctly. If you are on LinkedIn, Academia.edu, ResearchGate, Mendeley, or any other professional networking site, you should include links to your new publication.
2. **Make your work accessible**. If your publication is not open access, deposit an open access version to either your institution's own repository or another online repository after checking your publisher's copyright and self-archiving policies regarding sharing your published manuscript. You could also consider sharing your data to data-sharing websites such as such as figshare or SlideShare, or data repositories in your field.
3. **Follow up with your media relations office**. If you reached out to them prior to publishing, now is the time to follow up and let them know your work has been published.

Spreading the word and self-promotion

First, we think it is necessary to address the elephant in the room: self-promotion. This is a term that makes many people feel uncomfortable, especially newer researchers who may read the published work of those with titles such as 'Professor' and doubt that their work could ever be as worthy. We understand that promoting your research can feel uncomfortable and self-serving, but we urge you to take a different perspective on promoting research.

We have talked throughout this book about the reasons for publication, and for most researchers, these reasons include wanting to share your research with others in order to contribute to academic thought in your field, to inspire new ideas, to challenge conventional thought and in general to make a difference in this world. None of these aims can be met if your message does not reach the people who can use the information. Promoting your research is not making someone read it, use it or even like it. Promotion simply brings your publication into others' awareness in an age when it can be increasingly hard to identify critical research due to information overload. Carefully planned self-promotion benefits everyone: you and your readership. See Voice of Experience 10.2 for a Vice-Provost's advice on promoting your publications.

Voice of Experience 10.2

Advice on actively promoting your publications

Establishing yourself as a researcher can take years, and if you want to get your foot in the door, then it's helpful to look at the challenge from all angles. Getting noticed can only help, and you will get noticed if… you publish something cool. So, Golden Rule No. 1 – you must do something of genuine quality and substance that is worth noticing. What then? Well, a successful career will require you to repeat that success… so volume does matter – and getting enough 'mass' together at an early stage demonstrates your energy – so think about how you get more publications quickly too.

This is all about balance, and maybe this latter strategy, we might argue, is not ideal as a value proposition for a whole society, but heh, I am a pragmatist: this is how the system works. So, quality first, then think about the 'mass' to balance it up. And 'mass' often forces you into virtuous behaviours, such as collaborating – contributing your USP to someone else's project and publication (a win-win for you both) – or making a scary trip outside your comfort zone to your supervisor's international household-name collaborator and getting something extra, and publishable, done.

OK, so armed with some raw material, why is there the need to promote? Well, if your work is that good, in a field that is that big… sit back and relax! Good for you. But for many of us, we are a little more off the beaten track – but still part of a community of scholars. You want to become known in this community for all the right reasons – quality of your work, original thinking, accuracy, attention to detail, high-quality production, rigour in referencing – and as a contributor to the community – great posters, informative flash poster presentations, well-prepared conference talks with excellent slides, open, transparent and reliable collaborator, and as someone who says yes and delivers – e.g. journal or conference referee.

So, think about getting noticed – at every step along the way. Seek out the funding to go to the conference, once you have material ready to present, tick the box 'oral or poster', and accept the offer to do a flash poster. Just last week, at a conference I was confronted by a researcher who re-introduced himself to me and asked if I would visit his poster – slightly bemused, I did so, and will now remember him for some time to come. This is a good thing.

And then, when to create a web presence such as a Google Scholar page? Well, it does need some items, but as soon as you've published a few things, then why not? People can then establish at a keystroke who you are and whether they think you are ready to review that manuscript that cites your paper; otherwise, you remain a mystery, a little vacuum of information around you – and we all know about nature and vacuums.

And a final note on self-promotion – yes, you must believe in the quality of what you have got to sell, and that can be tough with less experience. In that, you need to trust that you have chosen a supervisor and project with the wherewithal. But, if you believe in yourself and your work, then self-promotion is a good thing – when in balance. It's all about the balance, but if your work 'has a heart', then the world needs to know about it, and you need to help the world with that.

See also my blog: https://blogs.surrey.ac.uk/vice-provost/2018/05/16/how-do-people-find-out-about-your-research/

Prof David Sampson, Vice Provost, Research and Innovation

While your publication may have an initial marketing push by the publisher, you will be responsible for maintaining further promotion. Thus, you will probably serve as the primary promoter of your work. If you are not used to promoting yourself or your work, this might take some practice. There are some quick, easy ways that you can practise this new skill. You can, for example, provide a link to the publication or to your publication record in your email signature. For a book, your publisher will probably have a banner you can use to draw attention to the signature section of your email. This is a simple way to tell those contacting you that you are published and to give them access to your publications.

Another way is to talk to other researchers about your publications. Remember to have copies of them displayed in your office, in break rooms, on department boards, and in offices near you. You can take this further and email copies or flyers to a list of researchers you think may be interested. Of course, another simple way is to cite your work, when it is relevant, in a new publication. However, it is important that you do this responsibly and not simply in order to increase your citation count.

Using social media

Social media offers a vast number of opportunities to promote your publications, in fact, so many that it may be overwhelming. Our advice is to think about what you want to achieve from social media and be selective in how you use it. Most social media platforms only work well for self-promotion if you are dedicated to maintaining your online readership. This will take a level of commitment, so unless you are already using the platform regularly, you should consider how much time and effort it will take to start using it effectively and pick the best option for you. Do not try to do everything all at once. Information Box 10.1 outlines some social media options and their respective strengths and weaknesses.

Information Box 10.1

Some social media options

Google Scholar

Strengths: (1) It is easy to use. You can set up an account and your publications can be available in 5–10 minutes. (2) It does not take a great deal of upkeep. You simply need to ensure that your publication record is accurate. (3) It has a feature that recommends papers to you. You can look at what they are recommending and ensure your articles have features, such as keywords, that will maximise the chances of those articles being recommended to others.

Weaknesses: (1) The automatic publication function does not always work, so you may need to delete publications that are not yours and add others that it did not find. (2) It is not as good at automatically finding books and chapters as it is for finding articles.

Twitter

Strengths: (1) It has a broad reach. (2) You can work on building up your followership in communities that contain your target audience by following and tagging organisations and members of those communities. (3) Each post is quick and easy to do.

Weaknesses: (1) It takes long-term commitment to build up a tailored followership. (2) It is not effective without a good followership. (3) Some audiences will not be on Twitter.

LinkedIn

Strengths: (1) It is very easy to build up a specifically-tailored followership. (2) It is quick and easy to post on. (3) Less continual posting is needed compared to other options, although the benefits of the platform will increase with the amount of effort you put in.

Weaknesses: (1) The audience is more specific than that of Twitter, primarily professionals. (2) It is more focused on individual self-promotion than research or work promotion. (3) To have full knowledge of who is interested in you or your posts, you must pay extra.

ResearchGate, Academia.edu, Mendeley

Strengths: (1) These options are easy to set up. (2) They do not take a high level of ongoing maintenance, although more interaction will increase benefits. (3) They are easy platforms for sharing publications.

Weaknesses: (1) The audience is primarily academic. (2) The choice between the above three options means some disciplines prefer one over the others, reducing the ability to share with interdisciplinary audiences.

Blog

Strengths: (1) This option gives you the space to explain why your research is important in more detail. (2) It enables you to use pictures or graphics to explain your work. (3) It allows you to write your message for specific audiences.

Weaknesses: (1) It takes time to write effectively, as it is essentially a lay publication. (2) It requires dedication to update the blog periodically in order to have significant impact. (3) You need to promote the blog to gain readership.

YouTube video

Strengths: (1) It caters to a broad audience. (2) Visual information is very accessible. (3) There is minimal ongoing commitment, although there is increased benefit from maintaining a YouTube channel.

Weaknesses: (1) It takes time and effort to plan well. (2) It requires expertise and technology to create high-quality videos. (3) Additional promotion is needed to maximise viewership.

No matter what social media platform you are using, you do need to consider your posts carefully. Ensure that you have the correct, live link to your publication. Consider tagging your publisher to tap into their network, or other researchers you think might be most interested in your work. Include relevant or trending hashtags that will get you recognised even by those who are not following you.

Although maintaining your own blog takes an ongoing commitment, you may want to consider writing a blog for your publisher, a professional organisation or another existing topic-focused site that your target audience is likely to read. Your blog can link to your article or book or link to your other social media accounts to generate more public engagement for your academic work. By doing this, you can reap the benefits of a blog and avoid some of the weaknesses.

We acknowledge that we have not covered all possible social media outlets and that perhaps even by the time of publication, there may be further social media options for researchers to use to promote their research. What we hope to achieve here is to give you a broad understanding of some of your options and to help you start to be able to assess the strengths and weaknesses of different options, taking into consideration the best ways in which to reach your specific target audiences. This is an important skill because virtual communication will continue to evolve and opportunities to promote your work will develop along with this evolution.

Getting your network to work for you

In our sister book, *Success in Research: Inspiring Collaboration and Engagement* (Reeves et al., 2020), we stress the importance of having a wide network and utilising that network to expand your opportunities. Your network can be advantageous for sharing and promoting your published work. If you are active on social media, for example, these are the people most likely to share, retweet, comment, like and so on your posts about your new publications. It is also worth appreciating the reciprocal nature of a collaboration network; if you share, like, retweet for others, they are more likely to do the same for you. In other words, investing time in promoting others' work will reap rewards for you too.

Conference attendance remains one of the most common and important ways to promote your work, as these are environments where our networks often come together face to face. For this reason, it is crucial to present your research within your academic discipline. Although most conference presentations do not usually count towards your academic publication record (except in a few specific disciplines), they will make your research more visible to the academic community. Presenting also has many added benefits beyond the promotion of your work, such as gaining new insights into trends in your fields, practising different ways of communicating your work more clearly and developing collaborations.

Conferences are also great opportunities to nurture and expand your network. By engaging with those already in your network, you will strengthen that connection and make it more likely that they will help promote and share your work. It is also worth building new connections, perhaps with those who have already cited your previous work, because those who cite you once are more likely to cite you again. You can bolster this likelihood by connecting more personally with those who cite your work. Seek them out at conferences or meetings. Every time you go to a conference, you should have at least one specific networking goal: to expand your connections. In Top Tips 10.3, we offer advice on how to promote your publications at your next conference.

Top Tips 10.3

Promoting your publications at conferences

1. Include notable publications in your conference biography if possible.
2. Use your talk as a taster. Do not give all the information included in your publication in your talk but encourage others to seek your publication for more details.
3. Pose questions to the audience to get their opinions and ideas on a topic.
4. Make networking goals and follow through.
5. Take copies of your publication, advertising flyers or copies of your abstract to hand out at the conference.

It may be good to expand your conference circuit and attend different conferences that attract a related but different target audience. If you do, remember you will have to adapt your key messages and your presentation style to suit this different audience.

The overall goal for promoting your research it to reach out to as many people as possible and to engage them with your research. Impactful research is research that attracts people from different audiences and helps them understand how your research can be useful to them. As you will see in the next chapter, this is what leads to more citations and, as we discuss in the final chapter, greater impact.

Further reading

AJE (2016) *AJE Scholarly Publishing Report: 2016* (Rep.). Durham, NC: American Journal Experts (AJE).

Ball, P. (2012) Rejection improves eventual impact of manuscripts. *Nature*, 11 October. doi:10.1038/nature.2012.11583

Calcagno, V., Demoinet, E., Gollner, K., Guidi, L., Ruths, D. and de Mazancourt, C. (2012) Flows of research manuscripts among scientific journals reveal hidden submission patterns. *Science*, 338(6110), 1065–1069. http://dx.doi.org/10.1126/science.1227833

Carrigan, M. (2016) *Social Media for Academics*. London: SAGE.

Corbyn, Z. (2010) An easy way to boost a paper's citations. *Nature News*. doi.org/10.1038/news.2010.406

Eveleth, R. (2014) Academics write papers arguing over how many people read (and cite) their papers. *Smithsonian Magazine*, 25 March. Retrieved from www.smithsonianmag.com/smart-news/half-academic-studies-are-never-read-more-three-people-180950222/

Reeves, J., Starbuck, S. and Yeung, A. (2020) *Success in Research: Inspiring Collaboration and Engagement*. London: SAGE.

11

How can you demonstrate and assess the impact of your publications?

Guest author: Alex Pavey

In this chapter you will:

- Be introduced to the key 'worlds' of bibliographic data and the different types of metric used in research assessment
- Contemplate the strengths and limitations of different metrics from the perspective of the individual researcher
- Consider the importance of deploying metrics responsibly
- See how metrics can be used to establish specific and measurable objectives for the impact of your publications
- Be encouraged to continually assess and evolve your publication strategy using the insights metrics can provide

Making metrics work for you

For the researcher who is committed to producing impactful research, who has carefully considered the advice in the preceding chapters and has worked hard to put the best strategies into practice, there is another piece of the puzzle to be considered. What evidence can we find that all of our hard work has had an effect? Without that evidence, assessing how successful we have been in meeting our personal objectives presents a challenge. Just as importantly, we may struggle to demonstrate the impact of our research to those who fund us, directly or indirectly – our universities, our funding bodies and our governments.

Those institutions are themselves invested in looking for ways in which research impact can be quantified. To this end, metrics designed to evaluate research productivity and impact are being deployed, often with increasing sophistication, both within and outside academia. Within universities, departments, faculties and central services, senior management teams make use of metrics for assessing the strengths and weaknesses of their research outputs. In some cases, they also use them to assess individual researchers. Decisions about hiring or promotions, for example, may now be informed by some degree of quantitative assessment using various metrics. Indeed, in many fields this has been the norm for some time.

There are certainly reasons to welcome some of these developments. Decisions that were once made largely on the basis of qualitative assessment – perhaps at risk of reinforcing existing biases and prey to unexamined assumptions – can now take into account quantitative measures. These data, used sensitively, can in theory reveal previously unrecognised strengths in individual researchers, groups or departments; those assumptions and biases can now be challenged. Research that might once have been dismissed for failing to garner traditional marks of academic prestige can be shown to be highly relevant to other sectors of society (see Chapter 12 for more on the importance of wider dissemination).

This drive towards quantifiable impact is not without its critics, however, and any discussion of research metrics must acknowledge that it is controversial terrain. As researchers, we tend to place a particularly high value on our intellectual autonomy; we are also, by temperament, often high achievers with a tendency to demand a great deal of ourselves. Independent, highly motivated and rather self-critical, it is understandable that we might resent what we perceive as externally imposed mandates. It is also natural to feel uncomfortable when our scholarship can be ranked, judged and potentially found wanting on the basis of sometimes-opaque metrics and analysis.

In this chapter we will seek to demystify some of these issues and focus on the opportunities that metrics present for individual researchers seeking to demonstrate the impact of their research. However, we will do so with the acknowledgement that there are ways in which metrics can be stressful for researchers. Some of that stress can be alleviated through developing a better understanding of the commonly-used metrics and their limitations. We will seek to empower you to use metrics in a positive and productive way and identify some approaches that we feel are unhelpful or unnecessary. Used responsibly, they can be powerful tools that enable you to assess the strengths and weaknesses of your publication strategy. They can also help you identify new opportunities for networking and collaboration.

Introducing bibliometrics and altmetrics

Bibliometrics as a field is concerned with the quantitative evaluation of research outputs – it attempts to measure the impact of academic publications, and the productivity and effectiveness of both researchers and institutions. Traditional bibliometric analysis is grounded in the citations that individual publications receive, and so the measures used in this type of analysis are commonly referred to as *citation metrics*. Of course, by definition, these types of metric can only assess one form of impact: the extent to which your work has been cited by your peers in academic publications. The particular value of altmetrics, which we will discuss below, is that by drawing on a wider range of data sources, they have the potential to measure other forms of impact.

Data can be aggregated at different levels, depending on the analyst's objectives: the impact of a single publication can be assessed, or groups of outputs analysed to assess the impact of an individual researcher, a research group, a journal, an institution or even a country. As a researcher concentrating on maximising the impact of your own publications, the metrics you are likely to find most useful are *article-level metrics*.

Bibliometrics relies upon indexes of citations, drawn from academic journals and other publications, and collected in citation databases. There are three major citation databases: Scopus, Web of Science and Google Scholar. All three differ in the number of publications they include, and in the chronological depth and disciplinary breadth of their coverage. This has particularly significant implications when comparing citation counts and other metrics that are integrated into all three platforms. The h-index, for example, is a commonly-used metric for assessing the productivity and impact of individual researchers. Users can view a given author's h-index within Web of Science, Scopus and Google Scholar, but the author's h-index will usually differ in each database, based on differences in the number of texts indexed in each. Activity 11.1 will help you explore these differences.

Activity 11.1

Comparing citations on different databases

Choose two or three publications from established researchers in your field and a publication of your own if possible. Look up these publications in Web of Science, Scopus and Google Scholar, and compare the results. Do the publications appear in all three databases? Are the citation counts different in each database? In most cases, Google Scholar will give the highest citation count – did you find this to be the case?

Rather than attempting to provide an exhaustive list of research metrics – one which would date quickly, given the rate at which bibliometrics continues to evolve – in the following section we will introduce you to the most important categories of metric, before going on to consider how you can best make use of them.

Journal metrics

Journal-level metrics are best used to assess the impact of a specific journal or to facilitate comparison between journals. When you are planning your publication strategy, journal metrics can help inform your decision about where to submit your paper.

The most well-known of these are the Journal Impact Factors (JIFs) – Citescore, which is based on the Scopus database, and the SJR Impact Factor, which is integrated into Web of Science. As we will discuss below, the widespread use of Journal Impact Factors as a proxy for assessing the quality of individual papers has been the source of much debate among bibliometricians and researchers. As a result, various other journal-level metrics have been developed to complement JIFs, including the Eigenfactor, the SCImago Journal Rank (SJR), and the Source Normalized Impact per Paper (SNIP).

Author metrics

Author-level metrics attempt to quantify the productivity and impact of individual researchers by aggregating data related to their publications. They can be useful for giving you an indication of the overall academic impact you have made with your publications as your career develops.

The most straightforward author-level metric is the citation count, which is the total number of citations received by all publications attributed to you in a given database. As mentioned earlier, the h-index is probably the most well-known author metric within academia. It provides an indication of an author's impact based on the citation rates of their publications – the higher the h-index, the greater the academic impact achieved. The most important thing to remember about the h-index is that it is not normalised to account for differences between publication practices in different disciplines. A reasonably successful, but not exceptional, early-career researcher working in a field where high volumes of journal publications are the norm would likely have a significantly higher h-index than a research 'superstar' in parts of the arts or humanities. As a result, the h-index and any other non-normalised metric should never be used to make comparisons between researchers or outputs in different disciplines.

Article metrics and altmetrics

We have elected to consider article-level metrics (ALMs) and altmetrics together here because they are best understood as closely related, although not inter-changeable, terms rather than as entirely discrete categories.

Altmetrics describes new online data sources, beyond traditional measures such as citation counts, that can be used to measure impact. This includes social media discussion, blog posts and comments, online news media cover-age, and Wikipedia articles, as well as online page views of articles and down-loads of full-text PDFs. Several providers, including ImpactStory, Plum Analytics and Altmetric.com, aggregate altmetrics from these diverse sources to provide a richer view of research impact. Altmetrics drawn from these providers are increasingly being integrated into bibliometric tools that previously focused on citation impact metrics.

As a data source, altmetrics can be used to assess author and journal impact, but they are most closely associated with article-level metrics, since it is at the article level that altmetrics and traditional measures of citation impact can be combined most powerfully. It is also article-level metrics that are most useful for individual researchers who are striving to maximise the impact of their publica-tions. Article metrics can help you better understand the true reach and impact of your research: from the number of downloads your paper received in the first month it was available online and the types of discussion it prompted on Twitter, to the citations it accrued in the following two years and where your interna-tional academic audience is located.

Responsible metrics

Many audiences, from funding bodies and university management to individual scholars, have an interest in evaluating the quality of research outputs and the impact of researchers. As metrics for assessing the impact of research outputs have proliferated and become increasingly accessible since the early 2000s, bib-liometricians and other academics have sought to ensure such measures are used appropriately and responsibly.

The two most well-known attempts to formalise best practice in the use of research metrics are the San Francisco Declaration on Research Assessment, or **DORA**, published online in 2013, and the Leiden Manifesto for Research Metrics (*Nature*, 23 April 2015). In both cases, groups of researchers came together to establish principles for the responsible use of metrics and to warn against certain tendencies they judged to be unhelpful or misleading. Neither can be viewed as the last word on what is an ever-evolving field, but they are valuable statements of good practice with which all researchers should be familiar.

Common to both the Leiden Manifesto and DORA is their emphasis on the importance of using a range of appropriate metrics, alongside other contextual information, so that quantitative measures are used to inform qualitative assessments of research rather than being deployed in isolation. This principle is as relevant to individual researchers informally assessing their own work as it is to institutions making employment or funding decisions. If you find yourself getting preoccupied with your h-index or citation count at the expense of anything else, remind yourself that no responsible peer or employer would judge you in this way.

Within universities, bibliometrics specialists are likely to be the most vocal advocates for these responsible approaches to research assessment. They will frequently be involved in preparing reports that identify areas of research strength internally. Strategic funding bids will likely be bolstered by their analyses. Potential collaborations with research centres at other institutions may be identified through the benchmarking exercises they undertake. At the same time, they will often be instrumental in developing and revising best practices, engaging with their professional networks to build upon the principles of statements like DORA and the Leiden Manifesto, and influencing their institution's policy on metrics usage. It is always worth familiarising yourself with your current or prospective university's stated approach to metrics, because it can give you a clear indication of how research assessment is expected to be conducted by promotion panels and hiring committees. Activity 11.2 explores this idea further.

Activity 11.2

Metrics at your university

Universities are increasingly developing and publishing their own policies concerning the responsible use of metrics. Search for references to bibliometrics on the website of your current or most recent university. How much information about research metrics do they provide? Have they published guidelines on responsible metrics usage or committed to an institutional policy? Are they a DORA signatory?

What you can do to use metrics responsibly

Taking a responsible approach to metrics is not only a matter for university senior management or bibliometrics specialists writing policy documents. Individual researchers can and should also play a role, by being careful to avoid perpetuating unhelpful practice; indeed, one section of DORA specifically addresses the actions researchers themselves can take. Making unfair comparisons grounded in inappropriate or outdated metrics is one of the most important things to avoid, and this applies whether it is your peers or your own work that falls short in such comparisons.

There are several widely-known metrics that bibliometrics specialists would now only use very cautiously, if at all, in assessing researchers and outputs, but which still linger in discussions among researchers. One type of such metric is the Journal Impact Factors, or JIFs. JIFs are journal-level metrics that are calculated on an annual basis and are based on the mean citation rate of articles published in that journal during a given number of preceding years. As journal-level metrics, they are intended to be used as a means to compare different journals, assessing their relative impact using the traditional measure of academic citations. Indeed – and as the DORA statement explicitly highlights – the impact factors were originally conceived as a way for publishers to market their journals to university libraries, and certainly not as a way to assess the quality of the research within the journals.

Even on these terms, JIFs have their limitations. Because they are calculated based on the mean citation rate of all papers published in a given journal, a handful of very highly-cited papers can skew a journal's results significantly. Moreover, certain types of paper, such as review articles, tend to be heavily cited. Journals that frequently publish such articles, or that strategically adjust their editorial policy to favour them, can give the impression of having a disproportionately higher impact.

Perhaps the most significant consideration is that any journal-based metric, by its nature, is unable to directly assess the quality of an individual output or researcher on their own merits. Yet, there has been a tendency in the past for journal impact factors to be used as a proxy measure for the quality of individual papers within a given journal, and it is this practice that DORA, for example, actively discourages.

This is not to say that you should avoid journals with high impact factors when planning your publication strategy. The most prestigious journals in their fields, with highly rigorous peer review processes and large international readerships, do tend to have consistently higher impact factors. Aspiring to be published in such a journal is a rational objective, and success can be a significant or even essential step in a researcher's career. However, given the now widespread availability of article-level metrics, Journal Impact Factors should play a very limited role when you are assessing your own post-publication research impact.

Limitations of traditional metrics for early-career researchers

Even some of the more rigorous, normalised author-level metrics can fail to do justice to the potential impact of early-career researchers. This is because most of these metrics are based upon *volume* – the number of publications that an individual has authored and the number of citations they have received. They are fundamentally most reliable and informative when these numbers are higher. Established researchers may have several productive decades behind them, and dozens or hundreds of publications that have accrued citations throughout that time. Early-career researchers, by definition, will not.

Given the above factors, it is very important for early-career researchers to be aware that there are limits to how much they should be concerned about their individual citation counts and metrics. Recognise the role that metrics play within institutions, but do not use them as an excuse to be self-critical or to contrast your achievements negatively with your peers. Treat them as a tool and think about how you can make them work for you. First and foremost, undertake innovative research that you are passionate about. Then, use metrics to help you develop, assess and refine your publication strategy to maximise your impact.

Using metrics to assess and evolve your publication strategy

A good publication strategy will constantly evolve over the course of what will, hopefully, be a long and successful career in research. Much of that evolution will be driven by developments in your research itself. For example, securing a post-doctoral position to investigate viral pathogens in poultry, having previously worked on the detection of infections in human subjects, might lead to an unexpected specialism in veterinary medicine. The Geographic Information System (GIS) mapping skills developed during a doctorate on literary geographies might be the inspiration for a new project positioned decisively within the digital humanities. A particularly significant set of results might lead you to targeting your next publication at the most selective and prestigious journal in your field, or raise your expectations for how much impact the research could have on government policy. All of these hypothetical situations, and the innumerable others that you may encounter in your career, would lead you to refine your approach to publishing your research.

Changes in your publication strategy should also be informed, however, by you reflecting on the goals you have previously set for yourself – assessing where you have met your objectives, where you have not, and how your approach could be altered fruitfully. This is an area where metrics can be hugely valuable to the individual researcher; they are a source of quantitative data that you can use to assess your existing strategy and to refine your future publication plans.

For this reason, you should ensure that all the objectives you set for yourself are **SMART** – Specific, Measurable, Achievable, Relevant, Time-bound. If you are clear about what you hope to achieve, the quantitative data accessible using bibliometric tools can provide a clear picture of the extent to which those goals have been met.

Of course, when you are still relatively early in your research career, it is not always obvious what a set of appropriate and realistic objectives for your publications might be. How many citations should you be aiming for? How many times does your article need to have been downloaded for you to consider it impactful? Metrics can help with this process too, by giving you an informed picture of what 'success' looks like. Most importantly, they allow you to base your understanding on up-to-date measures within your own field, and among researchers at a similar career stage to your own. Hearing second-hand that a colleague averages 2,000 citations per year is not a particularly useful data point against which to measure yourself, particularly if they are an eminent professor in the medical sciences and you are a post-doc on a social science project.

Benchmarking yourself

You can use benchmarking to provide a clearer picture based on relevant metrics within your discipline. To do this, begin by identifying a range of researchers in your field at different career stages, from 'research superstars' and eminent professors, through mid-career researchers with several projects under their belts, to post-docs and other researchers at the earliest stage of their research career.

Use contextual information to inform your selection. If you are jointly authoring a paper with your project's **Principal investigator** (PI), are you aware of another academic in your field who is at a similar career stage to your PI? Using a combination of article metadata and information from their university's website, find the names of post-docs working on this academic's project. Consider peers you have met at conferences who are working on similar topics. If you are a PhD candidate, look at other doctoral researchers and post-docs in your department or research group.

Once you have compiled a list of researchers, look up each of them on the same citation database and compare their author- and article-level metrics; creating a spreadsheet and pasting in information will help you keep track of your data. Looking at your results, ask yourself these questions:

- What level of publication impact would be unrealistic to expect at my current career stage, but might be realistic to achieve in five or 10 years' time?
- For someone in my position, what level of impact should I expect to achieve as a minimum measure of success, and beyond this what would be an ambitious but still attainable goal?

If you followed this approach, you might draw up a list of objectives for a new paper that looked something like this:

- To be cited at least once by members of each of the six other research groups known to be working on a closely related topic, within 12 months of publication.
- To receive at least x citations in the first two years.
- To demonstrate international impact through at least 40% of citations coming from researchers based in other countries.
- To attract readers from a broader disciplinary base, receiving at least 300 full-text downloads and citations from at least three journals outside your specialist area.

Building on the advice in the preceding chapters, you should be able to plan an approach with the best chance of meeting these objectives. Once the article has been published, and sufficient time has passed, you can use article-level metrics to help you assess whether each of these objectives has been met.

Always remember that, along with maximising the potential impact of your publications, committing to this kind of strategic approach has other benefits. Picture a fellowship panel asking you how well your work has been cited. Anyone could answer by reeling off a few citation numbers and trying to defend them or place them in context. But what if, instead, you could explain how you met each of the specific objectives you had set for your most recent article, which were informed by an assessment of your previous publications and benchmarks within your field, and how this would influence your goals for future work? That information would demonstrate your knowledgeability, motivation and ambition.

Finding your 'might reads'

In Chapter 1, we discussed how one of the most important parts of a successful publication strategy is identifying your potential audience. If your goal is to increase the impact of your publications, it is vital that you plan to expand your audience beyond your 'will read' – those who will inevitably read your work because it relates closely to their own research – and reach those who might read your work. Finding your 'might reads' requires reflection, creative thinking and a careful, tailored approach. Who are your potential audiences and what tactics might be best employed to reach all of them? These are challenging questions, and no researcher is likely to answer them, successfully and definitively, with their first publication.

One of the opportunities that bibliometric tools offer is the ability to identify your actual audience. Citations can be analysed by discipline, by country and by institution. Readerships can be quantified; comments on social media and blogs can be measured. As such, metrics can provide a clear indication of how effectively you have reached your potential audience with each publication, and they can inform your strategy for future activity. This will allow you to evaluate your identification of 'might reads'.

Metrics cannot give you all the answers; like all data, they need to be analysed rigorously, and this analysis should form part of a holistic assessment of your research strategy. For example, metrics alone cannot tell you whether you only received a limited response from a certain audience because your strategy for reaching that audience could be improved, or because you overestimated the extent to which that audience would be interested in your results.

Beyond providing you with the means to assess how successfully you met your previous objectives, metrics can also help you set future objectives in a more informed way. If you receive a cluster of citations from researchers in a field that surprises you, or from a country you did not think would have much interest in your results, then you have identified a new set of 'might reads' that you had not previously considered.

Unexpected citations like this can be valuable in developing your future research and publication strategy. Are there conferences or journals to which you could submit in future? Are there potential collaborators in other fields? Could you approach someone in another discipline who has cited your work positively? Where might that approach lead? Are there possibilities for a co-edited essay collection, a jointly-authored paper, an invitation to co-convene a conference or speak at a departmental seminar? Activity 11.3 will help you think about these opportunities.

Activity 11.3

Examining others' citations for patterns

On Google Scholar, look up some of the publications you have referred to in your research. Identify several that have been cited at least 25 times. Browse through the list of citations. Are all the publications that cite the original work familiar to you, or from journals you would expect? Are there any citations that particularly surprise you? Look out for examples of citations from adjacent fields, or from disciplines you might think of as unrelated to that of the original research. Establish why the original publication has been cited in these places by looking at those unexpected citations. Was the research method applicable in another context? Did the results have implications for another field of inquiry? Is the same topic being explored, but in radically different ways, in other disciplines?

It takes time for citations to build up, and you should always account for this when using metrics to analyse your own output. Bear in mind that it is unlikely that this time frame will coincide precisely with when you are planning your next publication. Depending on how frequently publication is expected in your discipline, will you have authored several other publications before your first has been published long enough for you to be able to assess its citation impact? Do some planning for future citations by engaging with Reflection Point 11.1.

Reflection Point 11.1

Building a publication strategy incorporating citation timings

Based on your understanding of citation timings in your field, think about a suitable time frame for reviewing your citations and assessing the impact of one of your publications. How might you incorporate such milestones into your future publication strategy?

Using altmetrics as more immediate indicators of impact

One of the most attractive aspects of the various measures encompassed by the term altmetrics is their immediacy. For all kinds of user, from individual researchers to university management and funding bodies, altmetrics offer the promise of measuring the impact of publications in a much shorter time frame than it takes for traditional citations to accrue.

This immediacy can let you take a much more active role in responding to the impact of your publications. You might notice that the blog post you wrote for your research group's website, which included a link to an open access version of your article, prompted an immediate, but temporary, spike in the number of reads and downloads the article received. Perhaps you could build on this by writing a follow-up post two months later, in which you update readers on how the project is continuing to evolve.

Some **altmetric aggregators** differentiate between the various types of engagement that a publication can prompt, and these distinctions can be particularly useful. ImpactStory, for example, distinguishes between 'reads', 'discussions' and 'recommendations'. If your article prompts a lot of discussion on academic blogs and social media, you could write a post for your personal website that collates those discussions and responds to the key questions raised by others.

Altmetrics can also be usefully deployed in other contexts, particularly by early-career researchers with fewer publications to their name. Publishers usually expect prospective authors to provide an indication of the potential market for a publication as part of a book proposal. Using altmetrics to demonstrate the international reach of your research, or its potential to engage non-specialist audiences, will help you to put forward a much more convincing and appealing proposal. Some more future planning is incorporated into Reflection Point 11.2.

Reflection Point 11.2

Using metrics in the future

Based on all of the above and informed by your understanding of the norms within your own discipline, think about how you can best make use of metrics in future. What are the most relevant measures of research impact for you? How might they change across the course of your career? How will you incorporate them into your publication strategy?

You should now be well placed to make use of metrics proactively when planning and assessing your publication strategy. Top Tips 11.1 provides a summary of key advice to bear in mind.

Top Tips 11.1

Incorporating metrics into your publication strategy

1. Be patient! Remember that several years are needed for an output to build up citations that are reflective of its impact.
2. Familiarise yourself with the full range of different metric types and what they measure.
3. Avoid misleading comparisons based on metrics taken from different databases.
4. Identify the metrics that are most appropriate for you based on your discipline and career stage.

5. Recognise the limitations of specific metrics, and of metrics in general – be clear what they can and cannot tell you.
6. Look to the future: try to identify opportunities for future collaborations when assessing how your publications have been received.
7. Establish reasonable and relevant benchmarks for yourself.
8. Use metrics to measure your future success and to identify ways to improve further.
9. Be an advocate for responsible metrics among your peers.
10. Build a narrative around your research that is grounded in a range of different metrics and tell that story in applications, proposals and interviews.

You cannot control how others make use of metrics – whether that be hiring committees, departments or peers. You *can* control how you use them and your own attitude towards them. We strongly suggest that you do not spend excessive time comparing yourself with your peers, because there is always someone against whom you will fall short. Instead, pursue quality research and judge yourself against the objectives you have set for yourself. We believe that quantitative metrics should only be a secondary measure of something you will already be passionate about doing: undertaking vital research and disseminating it to the widest possible relevant audience.

Further reading

Hicks, D. et al. (2015) Bibliometrics: The Leiden Manifesto for Research Metrics. *Nature*, 520: 429–431. doi: 10.1038/520429a
San Francisco Declaration on Research Assessment. https://sfdora.org/read/
Sugimoto, C.R. and Larivière, V. (2018) *Measuring Research: What Everyone Needs to Know*. Oxford: Oxford University Press.
Wilsdon, J. et al. (2015) *The Metric Tide: Report of the Independent Review of the Role of Metrics in Research Assessment and Management*. doi: 10.13140/RG.2.1.4929.1363

12

How can your publications have influence and benefit beyond academia?

In this chapter, you will be introduced to:

- A range of reasons for conducting research
- The impact agenda
- The impact–publication nexus
- How you can make a difference and have influence beyond academia
- Publishing and promoting your research strategically

From publication to impact

Throughout this book we have consistently discussed the value of publication in terms of engaging various audiences with your research in order to extend knowledge, to educate, to collaborate and to influence. In the last chapter, we explored the various ways in which you can measure the usage of your publications, focusing on your academic publications. In this chapter, we will focus on the next step: the impact of your publication, that is, the actual benefit of your research. In other words, what has happened that would not have happened (at least not in the same way) if you had not done your research and communicated it to other people.

Our motivation to do research is often the mixture of a true passion for our research area, a desire to succeed in our profession and a desire to make a difference that can be evidenced in some way. It is frequently this goal of making a difference that sustains us in what can be a demanding and frustrating job. In short, we want our work to make an impact. Jennifer Chubb conducted her doctoral research into what this means to academics. She found a variety of responses, including a feeling of responsibility, a strong desire to make a difference in the world as well as some resistance to the expectation of impact, at least immediate impact (Chubb, 2017). In our sister book, we discuss similar questions to those posed by Dr Chubb (*Success in Research: Achieving Impact in Research*; Denicolo, 2014, Chapter 3), and these questions are summarised for you to consider in Reflection Point 12.1.

Reflection Point 12.1

What are your motivations for doing research?

We provided above a selection of potential reasons for conducting research. Do any of them resonate with you? Do you have other drivers? How do you know when those reasons or drivers have been satisfied? How do you demonstrate that satisfaction to others?

Interpretations of impact

When we compiled *Achieving Impact in Research* (Denicolo, 2014), the Impact Agenda was pervading academia in the UK, dominating debate. Some colleagues regretted what they perceived as a negative move, drawing resources (people and funding) away from 'blue skies' research, the outcomes of which may not be observable for years to come, and towards practical research with tangible outcomes being obvious immediately or soon. Others counter-argued that no one should want to do meaningless research and that impact need not lead only to applied research or experimental development because theoretical research can produce the impact of a contribution to knowledge, valuable in its own right and providing potential for future research and outcomes.

As time has passed, the more polarised views have faded somewhat as a need to justify the use of public funds has grown and as recognition has increased that research has both immediate and longer-term impacts, the latter being frequently unpredictable in nature and magnitude. The *Frascati Manual* (OECD, 2002) divides research into three activities: (1) basic research to achieve new knowledge, with no particular application or use in view, although it might well have in the future; (2) applied research to acquire new knowledge but directed towards a specific practical aim; and (3) experimental development, drawing on existing knowledge to produce new products, materials, processes or services, or to improve substantially those that already exist. Further, there is a recognition of other dimensions to impact both within the way it is formally measured for institutional and individual accreditation through such exercises as **Research Excellence Framework (REF)** in the UK and more generally globally (see the section on measuring impact). The main types of impact that might derive from your research are presented in Information Box 12.1.

Information Box 12.1

The main types of research impact

Academic impact: Composed of a demonstrable addition to what is known or a shift in understanding that advances theory and method.

Economic impact: Tends to be quantifiable although there are many possible variants that demonstrate an increase in revenue or profit or economic good, such as jobs or improved business practices.

Social impact: Covers a range of valuable contributions to society, including social welfare, social equity, improvements in public services and training of practitioners.

Environmental impact: Ranges from influence on environmental policy, to contributions which increase sustainability, encourage behavioural changes and reduce the pollution and consumption of natural resources.

Health impact: Includes contributions to clinical policy as well as lives saved and improvements to patient care and quality of life.

Cultural impact: Covers research that contributes to public engagement with the aim of developing public attitudes and practices through education about important issues.

What the list of potential impacts from research activity makes clear is that no impact can be achieved unless other people know about, and have access to, your research and its outputs/results.

What this means for your publication strategy

You will already be thoroughly aware, by this point in the book, that academic impact can be readily achieved through disseminating your research at conferences and through printed or electronic means such as papers/articles, monographs or books. We have also discussed other opportunities for impact generation, such as blogs and other electronic communications that draw attention to and promote your research. In turn, your own research ideas will have been stimulated by such material in all those recognisable conduits. These form the 'normal' circulatory system carrying the lifeblood of academic practice, ideas and information.

Some forms of impact, though, require both stimulation and dissemination from and to the world outside traditional academic practice. It means engaging with users, stakeholders and participants, to gain access to their worlds as you develop your research plan and as you conduct your research since they are the gatekeepers to essential knowledge. Then you must share your results with them in forms that are both accessible to, and readily used by, them (see Chapter 8). The UK Research and Innovation (UKRI) Economic and Social **Research Council** (ESRC) elaborate on this in Information Box 12.2.

Information Box 12.2

Factors that support impact

Some of the numerous factors that help generate impact include:

- Establishing networks and relationships with research users
- Acknowledging the expertise and active roles played by research users in making impact happen
- Involving users at all stages of the research, including working with user stakeholder and participatory groups
- Having flexible knowledge exchange strategies, which recognise the roles that partners and collaborators may wish to play
- Developing good understanding of policy/practice contexts and encouraging users to bring knowledge of context to research
- Being committed to portfolios of research activity that build up reputations with research users
- Working consistently towards excellent infrastructure, leadership and management support
- Involving intermediaries and knowledge brokers as translators, amplifiers and network providers at times
- Supporting space and time for collaborative reflection on research design and process, findings and overall progress.

See more here: https://esrc.ukri.org/research/impact-toolkit/what-is-impact/

These characteristics are developed over many years of research activity, aided by supportive institutional environments as well as considerable practice and reflection with colleagues and users.

It is only by such collaboration and engagement that your research can influence practice and thereby obtain measurable impact. (See our sister book, *Success in Research: Inspiring Collaboration and Engagement* (Reeves et al., 2020), for a detailed discussion of engagement.)

Influencing outside the academic sector

Influencing professional practice

Developing connections with professionals in other zones of activity can take researchers out of their comfort zone because it requires researchers to recognise that those other people have expertise different from, but complementary, to their own. Entering into the spirit of sharing expertise, ideas, challenges and solutions, and becoming less possessive of your usual way of doing things, will help with any discomfort you may feel in the forging of these connections. By opening your eyes to alternative perspectives and ways of operating, your own creativity can be enhanced, just as you can reciprocate by providing guidance and stimulation from a researcher's perspective to professional practitioners. Indeed, sometimes the greatest enjoyment, as well as revelatory ideas, come from such disturbance to our usual way of doing things, as we evidenced in Voice of Experience 12.1.

Voice of Experience 12.1

How to fulfil your passions through considering others' needs

My research passion has always been two-fold: understanding how others perceive their worlds and helping people to learn to see their worlds in ways that are more effective for them. My research focused, firstly, therefore, on constructivist research in a wide range of education settings. However, I found that fellow researchers valued my expertise in methodology, so I found myself working and writing with, for example, professionals-as-researchers involved in:

- care for the elderly, exploring older persons' values that superseded their concern for their own health and safety;
- coral reef conservation, investigating fisherfolks' concerns about sustainable fishing techniques;
- palliative care, studying Asian views about illness and dying;
- One Health, surveying beliefs about links between environmental, animal and human health;
- the mental health and welfare of first responders, a concern of the Emergency services.

All these topic areas were beyond my comfort zone of expertise, so I learned a lot as I engaged with them in Action Research. By and large the professionals had identified the problems to explore, but we refined the research questions together, then all contributed to the research design. I lent support to the data collection and analysis, and we co-authored papers and reports to funders. However, it is not just the joy of learning that was a significant outcome for me but, beyond that and importantly, I met some wonderful people whom I would otherwise have never known. Further, I published in journals, 'grey literature' and books well beyond my limited initial field. More importantly, I felt that I had something useful to contribute to the world beyond academia.

Professor Emerita Pam Denicolo

Influencing commerce and industry

When one is undertaking applied research, opportunities to turn your academic research into innovation and eventual economic impact are both more obvious and more frequent. This can be done either by collaborating with industrial/commercial partners, who will support the translation to market, or through directly creating a spin-out company. If this eventual product development is an option for your research, it is important to discuss this early with people who provide legal and patent advice within your university because such considerations may affect how you publish your academic work. For example, if key work has been published in the public domain, you will not be able to obtain a patent on it. Therefore, it is critical to understand patenting rules so that you can adjust your publication plan to enable both academic publication and eventual patenting of your innovation.

As with influencing professional practice, influencing commerce and industry by developing innovations requires you to work with people from different disciplines and sectors. Finding a partner company or business to work with to translate your research into innovation can be an important first step. The company will have insight into industrial/commercial requirements and their customers' needs, both of which will influence whether your venture is successful. Early understanding of these practical needs will allow you to adapt your research to generate real-world impact.

In our experience, researchers may underestimate their ability to contribute to innovation. For example, the high-level analytical and technical skills researchers have can often have more impact on industry than one might imagine. Therefore, engaging with a wider range of people can sometimes lead to impactful serendipity, as described in Voice of Experience 12.2.

Voice of Experience 12.2

An unlikely REF case study

My focus of research is quite far away from application. So, when I was invited to a meeting with a company to talk about a potential collaboration, I thought it was highly unlikely I would have much to contribute. However, I decided to go along as a favour to the colleague who invited me and out of curiosity.

To my surprise, within that first meeting, I found there was quite a bit of our knowledge, both discipline-specific and methodological, that would be quite useful to this company. We managed to obtain a small amount of internal funding to get a pilot project started, and then managed to win further funding aimed at university–industrial partnerships. This provided funds to hire a post-doctoral fellow to work on a collaborative project between myself and the company. Although this project was quite far away from the research that is the mainstay of my work, I found working with industry incredibly interesting and a nice balance to the unpredictability of totally blue skies research.

That first meeting was five years ago, and the collaboration is still going strong. I have two patents, and a product line on the market as a direct result of innovation derived from this partnership. Importantly, this research is now going to be used as a REF impact case study.

A Physics academic

Even if you are not looking for an innovation partnership, but prefer to create your own spin-off company, you will need a range of expertise to make this a reality. Successful academic spin-offs tend to have a heterogeneous board of directors, with people bringing different expertise to the venture, including technical, legal and business expertise (De Cleyn, 2015). If you are interested in the spin-off route, you will need to find good partners, ideally with complementary skills to those you possess. You will also need to gain an understanding of your potential customer base, who are unlikely to have had previous access to your ideas or research. Lay publication may be a way to start engaging with this audience and understanding how to best market your innovation for them (see Chapter 8). Most universities have central departments to help support new spin-off ventures based on academic research. We recommend that you get to know these valuable resources and take full advantage of their support; they may be able to help you find partners and also engage with potential customers.

Stakeholder and user engagement

Working with others beyond academia can present a steep learning curve for all participants. All must learn to trust and respect the one another, which can take time as they explore and negotiate attitudes and beliefs. All groups are protective of their own *modus operandi*, believing that these are the best and that others do not have the professional insight that has been accumulated over years using those methods. It is easy to forget that blinkers have been accumulated as well. This includes blindly accepting the status quo or favouring traditional approaches, the rationales for which have long since been forgotten. It sometimes takes a naïve question, or an innocent remark, to make us notice things we take for granted that may or may not be important, or at least not as important as we previously assumed. In explaining to others, we come to know our own practice and concepts better, which can help us to challenge the implicit and contemplate alternatives.

Such explaining raises another crucial issue for those adventuring to do research with others beyond the boundaries of academia: language. The old saying about Americans and British people being divided by a common language applies equally to professional groups, whether they are based in different disciplines or different sectors of society, business or industry. When those from other professions invite us into their worlds, it behoves us to learn how they use language: the different uses of the same words, the different words for the same things, their language register, and so on. As discussed in Chapter 8, we tend to use a very arcane register in academia, and we should remember that, just because someone is not familiar with a word – **epistemology**, for instance – does not mean that they cannot understand the concept – in this case, a theory about knowledge. They, too, can distinguish between justified belief and opinion.

Thus, there is a need to communicate as clearly as we can, without being patronising, challenging our own as well as others' assumptions, and learning how to interact in their culture. This is especially important while negotiating and conducting joint research, but also when disseminating it. To reach a professional audience and to have impact on practice, we must engage with that wider profession or group in ways other than through academic journal articles that they have no reason to access, far less any opportunity to do so.

Publication choices

Of course, it is in your professional interest as a researcher to publish in academic journals to ensure that fellow researchers can learn from, emulate and challenge your research. Equally, if your co-researchers and professional partners are also doctoral researchers, they too will want to add to their academic credibility by publishing in the relevant discipline journals. However, will such publications influence practice in the context in which you collected data? While you are embedded in a new context and culture, it is worthwhile noticing and exploring which information sources are used by participants. They may subscribe to a magazine or newsletter related to their business, work or profession. They may access blogs or websites devoted to their interests. This is the 'grey literature' or lay publication (see Chapter 8) referred to in Voice of Experience 12.2 above. They may have regular updating or **continuous professional development** (CPD) meetings or workshops to which you could contribute.

What is most important is that you consider the kinds of impact your research could possibly make, which may be more than one of those listed in Information Box 12.1, and then find the best means of ensuring that your outputs become outcomes in the relevant sphere of life through active communication with potential users. We discussed this in detail in Chapter 8, specifically Activity 8.2.

Knowing that there are others out there who would be interested in your work is not enough. You cannot simply wait for serendipity to provide invitations for you to work, research and publish with others; you need to be strategic if you are going to turn publication into impact.

Measuring impact

In Chapter 11, we discussed measuring the success of your publication strategy in terms of academic usage of your work, as measured by a variety of metrics. Just as there is an increasing push to measure the academic impact of publication with metrics, there are similar pressures to measure the non-academic input of academic publications. As we learnt in the last chapter, measurements of academic impact are vastly complicated, but it is even more complex to attempt to measure the variety of different types of non-academic impact.

The UK Research Excellence Framework (REF), which assesses the research quality of UK universities, first included a measure of non-academic impact in 2014. To measure this type of impact, universities were asked to submit case studies that included underpinning publications, and a narrative case study describing the impact and how it was achieved. All of the 2014 REF impact case studies are now freely accessible and provide an interesting perspective on understanding the journey from research publication to research impact: https://impact.ref. ac.uk/casestudies/. Activity 12.1 challenges you to explore case studies within your field.

Activity 12.1

Exploring REF impact case studies

Go to https://impact.ref.ac.uk/casestudies/. Choose the Unit of Assessment that matches your area of research. On the right-hand side, go to the drop-down menu for 'types of impact' and observe the various types that were submitted. Choose one of the impact types to explore and read through a few of the case studies.

Questions to consider:

- How big was the 'reach' of this impact? (that is, how many people, animals or organisations, etc. were affected?)
- Do the authors provide strong evidence that their actions directly influenced this impact?
- Was it clear how the underpinning research led to this impact?
- Were there interdisciplinary, **intersectoral** and/or international collaborators involved?
- How did they communicate/work with their stakeholders?

This bank of impact case studies is an interesting dataset detailing the various ways that research can have impact and how researchers can evidence this impact. While the assessment of research impact may be controversial, especially with regards to the effect these measures have on individuals' career and research choices, understanding how you can achieve positive real-world benefit from your research, and how you can demonstrate this benefit, will be important for researchers for the foreseeable future. Therefore, it is worth taking some lessons from the REF exercise and thinking about how these can be used to your advantage.

The first striking observation we have when going through REF case studies is the importance of crossing traditional boundaries. Many of the case studies are derived from published work that involved interdisciplinary and/or international collaboration. The need to engage beyond academia is also apparent. The narratives detail policy papers, public engagement activities, professional workshops, co-patents with industrial partners, to name but a few examples. No doubt when you did Activity 12.1, you found evidence for this **boundary-crossing** engagement. Probably also, for many of these case studies, an element of serendipity played a part, as it did in the one described in Voice of Experience 12.2. This does not mean, though, that all impactful research comes about by chance. Far from it. You can proactively seek ways to engage these broader audiences with your publications and with your research, as discussed further in the next section. The challenge for academics to benefit the world positively and to demonstrate that benefit is here to stay; indeed, impact remains a key component of the 2021 REF (see Information Box 12.3). It is up to you to take up this challenge and make it an opportunity to excel in your career and to change the world for the better.

Information Box 12.3

REF 2021 Impact Case Studies Guidance

For the purposes of REF 2021

Impact includes, but is not limited to, an effect on, change or benefit to:

- the activity, attitude, awareness, behaviour, capacity, opportunity, performance,
- policy, practice, process or understanding
- of an audience, beneficiary, community, constituency, organisation or individuals
- in any geographic location whether locally, regionally, nationally or internationally.

Impact includes the reduction or prevention of harm, risk, cost or other negative effects.

Impacts on students, teaching or other activities both within and/or beyond the submitting HEI are included.

Academic impacts on research or the advancement of academic knowledge (whether in the UK or internationally) are excluded.

Impacts will be assessed in terms of their 'reach and significance' regardless of the geographic location in which they occurred, whether locally, regionally, nationally or internationally. The UK funding bodies expect that many impacts will contribute to the economy, society and culture within the UK, but equally value the international contribution of UK research.

(Full guidance can be found: www.ref.ac.uk/media/1092/
ref-2019_01-guidance-on-submissions.pdf)

Strategic routes to impact

When policy makers introduced the impact research agenda, their intent was to encourage researchers to make conscious efforts to ensure that their research made a 'real-world' difference. Further, the notion of **knowledge exchange** emerged to frame the processes by which academic research could encompass the two-way process: a need in the community stimulates research, which in turn contributes outputs in the form of policy, services, products and new perspectives. Working with user groups or public sector and business organisations that complement your disciplinary work in any way can have enormous benefits, such as additional experience and knowledge of contextual problems, additional funding and other resources. However, access to those benefits comes at the cost of time and energy spent in building the trusting relationship we introduced earlier.

You must plan for success in your collaborative work by first identifying potential stakeholders, then exploring their motivations and interests. You can then establish alignments between your perspectives and work together to design your future interactions, including dissemination. We have provided Top Tips 12.1 to help you with this process.

Top Tips 12.1

Planning your strategic engagement

1. Consider carefully who your external partners could be. You might start by checking with colleagues who they have worked with or are still engaged with, making sure that you do not upset any ongoing networks. It may be best to consider similar organisations rather than the same ones in the first instance or to ask your colleagues to introduce you to their contacts simply to seek their advice on other potential partners.
2. Prepare a succinct, jargon-free outline of your reasons for wanting to work with such partners, including benefits that could accrue to all parties and how your proposal is unique.
3. Through direct contact or online searches, identify a key contact by name and make your 'pitch'.
4. Do not be disappointed if you receive a negative response but ask that contact to suggest others from the sector who might be more interested/available. You may even get a personal introduction. Remember that the key attributes of a good researcher are persistence and resilience.
5. When you have successfully established a link, work with the partners to ensure that everyone will gain from the liaison.
6. Decide on mutually acceptable and convenient aims and objectives. A memorandum of understanding is a useful way of ensuring agreement, although it has no legal standing.
7. Establish clear lines of communication between a direct, identifiable person in your organisation and one in theirs who will be responsible for maintaining communications. Include regular contact dates so that you all have recognised reporting deadlines.

(Continued)

8. Ensure that agreement is obtained and maintained about terms of contract, costs and who pays them, copyright and patent issues, authorship order and royalty payments for any ensuing publications.
9. In terms of authorship order, consider which person will attract the highest readership figures (for further dissemination), will make the most 'impactful' use of your outputs, and will benefit the most from the publication. Achieve a fair balance with this.
10. Complete the process by leaving your partners with the sense of a successful encounter and a willingness to engage further with academia.

Working in this way establishes networks for you and your colleagues to benefit from in the future. A successful project will not only provide useful outputs directly from the research but will also introduce you to novel means of promoting your research, as discussed in Chapter 10. These are likely to then provide network links for future research.

Post-publication engagement

One of the joys of engaging in research with other communities is that it is not only the immediate co-researchers and participants who join your network. In addition, their networks become, with a little effort and some thoughtfulness, amalgamated with your own, to everyone's benefit, as is illustrated by our own recent experience, described in Voice of Experience 12.3.

Voice of Experience 12.3

Practice what you preach

As we wrote this book, an example arose in our practice. We had written a book for a specific group of professionals about developments in their practice and had delivered flyers to various venues that we visited in the following year. One person then suggested to their professional body that we might give a talk based on that book to an annual meeting. We agreed to do that, thinking that it would be interesting to get further feedback on our findings and perhaps also some additional data, and so the talk was advertised within that professional sector.

A bi-weekly professional newspaper picked up on that advertisement and asked if we could provide an illustrative segment of our talk for the next edition. We quickly put together a piece, wanting to oblige but being pushed for time, as ever. When it was published, we discovered that an advertisement had been added to our article, recommending not just the talk, but also the book. That, we felt, was a nice result: more participants and more readers. However, it did not end there.

> We heard of and received tweets and blogs, commenting on the work, the talk and the book – the ripples had spread afar and others, both in academia and the specific sector, joined in the e-discussion. This then resulted in more invitations to engage in collaborations in several ways with others interested in the research topic.
>
> *Dawn C. Duke, Pam M. Denicolo and Erin Henslee*

Most of those 'publications' emerging from the work in Voice of Experience 12.3 were not in high-esteem journals, nor will they make us a fortune as best-selling authors, but the transmission and elaboration of ideas that ensued certainly indicate a high degree of impact in terms of the meaningfulness and usefulness of the research we conducted. Indeed, it is the more informal versions of the dissemination and feedback we received that gave us the most enjoyment and fulfilment. Others' enthusiasm has fuelled our own.

Throughout this book we have tried to emphasise that sharing your work and research interests with others through diverse publication and dissemination routes not only adds to your own satisfaction with it, but can inspire you to research and write more, adding to your personal and professional impact. We wish you joy with it.

Further reading

Chubb, J.A. (2017) *Instrumentalism and epistemic responsibility: researchers and the impact agenda in the UK and Australia.* Unpublished PhD thesis, University of York.

Copley, J. (2018) Providing evidence of impact from public engagement with research: a case study from the UK's Research Excellence Framework (REF). *Research for All*, 2(2): 230–243. https://doi.org/10.18546/RFA.02.2.03

De Cleyn, S.H. (2015) How human capital interacts with the early development of academic spin-offs. *International Entrepreneurship and Management Journal*, 11(3): 599–621.

Denicolo, P.M. (ed.) (2014) *Success in Research: Achieving Impact in Research.* London: SAGE.

OECD (2002) *Frascati Manual: Proposed Standard Practice for Surveys on Research and Experimental Development.* The Measurement of Scientific and Technological Activities. Paris: OECD Publishing. https://doi.org/10.1787/9789264199040-en. www.oecdbookshop.org/oecd/display.asp?lang=EN&sf1=identifiers&st1=922002081p1

Reeves, J., Starbuck, S. and Yeung, A. (2020) *Success in Research: Inspiring Collaboration and Engagement.* London: SAGE.

REF2021 (2019) *Guidance on Submission.* www.ref.ac.uk/media/1092/ref-2019_01-guidance-on-submissions.pdf.

Ross, F. and Morrow, E. (2015) Mining the REF impact case studies for lessons on leadership, governance and management in Higher Education. LSE Impact of Social.Sciencesblogs.lse.ac.uk/impactofsocialsciences/2016/06/08/leadership-governance-and-management-research-mining-the-ref-impact-case-studies/.

Tanner, S. (2016) *An Analysis of the Arts and Humanities Submitted Research Outputs to the REF2014 with a Focus on Academic Books: An Academic Book of the Future Report.* London: King's College London. https://doi.org/10.18742/RDM01-76.

APPENDIX A

Concerns about open access to publications and responses to them

Concerns about open access to publications and responses to them	
Open access is too expensive	Paying a fee to publish open access is not the only option. Publishing in a journal that allows you to share your paper online (Green open access) is a very widely adopted option. This costs you nothing and you do not rely on the publisher to post the work for you: you, or someone you delegate, can upload the paper in an open access repository.
	If you or your funder have a preference to publish open access, check if your funder and/or institution can cover publication fees.
Open access compromises the quality of the work	Open access is compatible with peer review. The paper is shared online *after* it has been peer-reviewed and accepted for publication. Open access is also compatible with emerging models of open peer review.
	In many disciplines there is, of course, an established practice of sharing pre-refereed papers, on their way to being published, to ensure early dissemination of the research. This has been the case in the physical sciences for decades; it is also encouraged in biomedical research and is common practice in some of the social sciences. In these cases, it is crucial to label the versions that you share.
	Another quality concern stems from the bad publicity attached to open access publishing in general. While there is growing anxiety about so-called 'predatory publishers', 'vanity presses' or 'pseudo-journals', the problem with these journals lies with their inefficient editorial processes, and not with whether they provide open access or not. Most open access publishers have sound peer-review and editorial processes in place.
Open access violates copyright	Open access is compatible with copyright law. Established open access models always rely on the consent of the copyright holder to share the work online. This is, in fact, why keeping at least some dissemination rights to our publications is crucial for this to happen.
	It is true that open access to arts outputs is complicated with respect to copyright. Performances, for example, have multiple copyright owners. In this case, sharing is still possible if all copyright owners agree.

(Continued)

Concerns about open access to publications and responses to them

Open access undermines journals	Open access does not undermine journals, but it does put pressure on them to rethink and transform their current business models and the services they provide. In the online era, current production costs of electronic articles are increasingly hard to justify. So are the services journals provide, most of which, with the exception of peer review, may no longer be necessary if authors post their publications online. Open access initiatives call for the development of innovative, transparent and sustainable publishing models. It is important to note also that peer reviewers are not paid for their services.

Concerns about open access to theses

A journal may not accept my article if it is based on a thesis I have made public online	There is evidence that this is rarely the case: most publishers consider journal articles deriving from a thesis as substantially different from the thesis, and do not consider the thesis to be a prior publication. However, if you plan to publish in a particular journal and you have concerns, it is worth looking up the journal's relevant policy on the publisher's website or clarifying directly with the editor.

What is not best practice is restricting access to the thesis *just in case* publishers object to publication. Check with the journal and, often, you will be pleasantly surprised that this is not a problem. |
| **Sharing a thesis online means I will not be able to publish it as a monograph** | You may be right to be concerned about this. If you plan to publish the thesis as a monograph, it is advisable to check with your publisher.

Having said that, there is growing evidence that many publishers would not refuse to publish your thesis, as they would expect the material to be adapted and restructured substantially. |
| **Sharing a thesis online violates intellectual property/may compromise commercial interests** | This is a valid concern if the thesis contains any material that has commercial potential, for example, findings leading to the development of a patent or a creative writing thesis that can be published as a novel.

In many cases your doctoral research may also be sponsored by an organisation that owns any commercially sensitive material in the thesis. In these cases, you may have to restrict the thesis, at least for a specified period (embargo). If in doubt, speak to your university's intellectual property officer and/or your sponsor.

As for copyrighted material: if you are concerned about sharing copyrighted material in the thesis, for example, images or graphs not created by you, you should get permission from the copyright holder to include them. |
| **Sharing a thesis online is against data protection** | The main body of your thesis should not contain confidential/sensitive information. If this is part of your research, it should be included in a separate volume that is restricted. Alternatively, you could share a redacted version of the thesis. It is worth checking what your university's policy is on this. |
| **Sharing a thesis online before its content is published may mean others can plagiarise the content – or even publish this research before I do** | • Theses are automatically protected by copyright law.
• Research available online can be plagiarised, in the same way that work in print can be plagiarised. The difference is that plagiarism of online work will be easier to detect.
• Many doctoral students and their supervisors feel uncomfortable sharing research designs, ideas and findings before they are formally published. However, if anything, sharing the work online should spark interest and increase readership rather than urge others to carry out and publish the same research.
• It is true that in some cases the timing of sharing new research is crucial. This may be, for example, when the work would have greater impact if it were communicated publicly upon publication or is part of a larger project still in progress.
• For this reason, it is best to talk to any sponsors/collaborators and only restrict the thesis when you have a specific reason to do so. |

APPENDIX B

Routes to open access

	Gold open access	Green open access
Also known as	Open access publishing.	Author self-archiving.
Where do you publish?	• In an open access journal. OR • In a subscription journal offering an open access publishing option.	In a subscription journal.
Costs	Average cost is around £2,000 per article. This is called an Article Processing Charge (APC). However, some open access journals do not charge you to publish with them.	No open access fees. (Note that the journal may still charge you publication fees that have nothing to do with open access.)
Sharing the paper open access		
How does it work?	The paper is freely available on the publisher's website.	On the journal's website, the paper is only available to subscribers AND You share the accepted version of your paper online.
What can you share?	The published version.	Usually the *accepted version*. A few publishers allow you to share the published version.
Where can you share it?	On the publisher's website. Usually on additional websites, depending on the publishing agreement/licence.	On your institution's online archive – known as 'open access repository'. In other designated open access repositories, e.g. PubMedCentral or arXiv. Usually *not* on commercial networking sites (e.g. ResearchGate, academia.edu).

(Continued)

	Gold open access	Green open access
When can you share it?	As soon as it is published online.	It varies. It can be as soon as it is accepted or published, although many major publishers impose embargoes ranging from six to 24 months.
Copyright		
Who owns the copyright?	Usually you, the author.	Usually the publisher. However, you keep the right to share your version online. This should be written into the copyright transfer agreement you sign when your paper is accepted.
How can others use your paper?	The paper is usually published under a public licence allowing its free distribution (usually a Creative Commons Licence). Depending on the type of licence, others may be able to re-share, adapt or even use the content commercially. In any case, they must always correctly attribute the work to you.	They can download and read the open access version, but usually they cannot adapt or re-use it in a commercial context.

Glossary

Academia.edu   An online platform for sharing academic papers.

Altmetric aggregators   Platforms that collect, compile and analyse altmetric data.

Altmetrics   Altmetrics stands for 'alternative metrics', which measure and monitor the reach and impact of research publication through online interactions, such as views, downloads and shares.

Assessment

> **Formative** Evaluation of a learner's comprehension, academic progress and learning needs in order to provide feedback and guidance to aid improvement. Normally this occurs in-process, although it can be used by examiners at the end of a doctorate to guide future learning.

> **Summative** Evaluation of a learner's progress at the end of a stage or a course in order to recommend onward progression to the next stage or an award to mark completion.

Bibliometrics   Statistical analysis of the use and impact of research publications, typically utilising citation rates and number of publications over defined periods of time.

Blind peer review   The process of assuring anonymity when professionals are assessing a peer's publication, in an attempt to reduce bias.

> **Single-blind** refers to the author not knowing the identity of the reviewer.

> **Double-blind** refers to neither the author nor the reviewer knowing the identity of the other.

Blog   Truncated from 'weblog', a blog is a discussion or informational website published online. Entries are in reverse chronological order, so that the most recent blog posts are typically at the top.

Boundary-crossing   Not restrained by imposed labels, within the context of this book it refers to crossing one or more of the following: discipline, national context or sector.

Collaboration   In the context of publication, writing a publication with another person or a group of people.

Commercial publishers   Any privately-owned publisher with the purpose of selling books for profit. While often contributing to academia, their primary interest tends to be more 'commercial'. Also known as **commercial press**.

Commissioning editor   A commission editor, sometimes known as an 'acquisitions editor', is the person responsible for finding and proposing new titles to a publisher.

Continuous professional development (CPD)   This entails reading, workshops or other training events, new experiences, and so on intended to keep a professional person's practice up to date.

Contribution to knowledge   A contribution to knowledge relates directly to the notion of 'original' research. What counts as original may be subtler than at first imagined. Generally, all research will be built upon a pre-existing body of knowledge. Thus 'original' will be defined less by a breakthrough in research and more in terms of a contribution to it. The contribution could be, for instance, the repetition of a previous experiment or study in very different circumstances; the re-application of a research question with a new method; a reinterpretation of a prominent theory or thinker, and so forth. In any case, the contribution is original if it in some sense adds to or even challenges a present body of knowledge. Thus, the concepts of 'original' and 'contribution' are relative, and their function is incremental.

Creative Commons licence   A copyright licence that enables the free distribution of an otherwise copyrighted 'work'. A CC licence is used when the author wants to give other people the right to share, use and build upon their work.

Critique   An evaluation that notes the quality aspects of a piece of work or area of study, including what was good and what could be improved.

Core   (1) The central or most important aspect, i.e. the core idea of the paper. (2) A required text for a taught course, i.e. this is a core textbook for Microbiology.

Deliverables   In the context of project planning, evidence of progress (a product) that is planned to be obtained by a specific time.

Discoverability   Discoverability in this context simply refers to how discoverable your work is on a search engine or commercial/library database. Using the key words of your research and subject area in the title of your work is likely to make it more discoverable.

DORA   San Francisco Declaration on Research Assessment (2013) is a statement with regards to how research should and should not be assessed with an emphasis on fairness to researchers.

Epistemology   The branch of philosophy concerned with the study of knowledge its nature, justification and rationality of belief. An individual's epistemology is what s/he believes are the limits of truth and proof and what is recognised as only opinion.

Ethical   Relating to the moral principles that guide and govern researchers' behaviour in the conduct of their research projects.

Feedback   The range of comments and recommendations provided by assessors or evaluators in response to a piece of work they have been asked to judge.

Freemium model   An open access model where the digital version is published in open access with enhanced digital versions or print-on-demand options, to subsidise production costs.

Free writing   A method of writing that requires the writer to write continuously for a period of time without judging the output.

Formative assessment   See **Assessment, Formative**

Four Star journals   The highest scoring journals on specific impact factors. See also **Quartile One journals**.

Gold open access   The practice of a publisher making a paper open access on the journal website, usually once the author (or the institution) has paid a fee.

Green open access   The practice of an author (or their institution) posting a peer-reviewed version of a journal paper, usually the author's accepted manuscript, in an open access repository.

HASS   Short version of Humanities, Arts and Social Sciences.

Hybrid journal   A subscription journal that offers a paid open access option.

Impact case studies   Narratives describing the the benefit that specific lines of research have had, which are submitted as part of the UK Research Excellence

Framework. The entire collection of these case studies is freely available online. https://impact.ref.ac.uk/casestudies/

Impact factor A bibliometric measure of citation rate for a group of publications. It can be applied to publications within a specific journal or to the publications of an individual, usually over a defined period of time for both.

Impostor syndrome A pattern of behaviour in which people doubt the value of their accomplishments, often feeling a fear of being exposed as a fraud.

Index An organised list of information, typically coming at the back of a book. It usually contains key terms, concepts and names used in a book with corresponding pagination.

Interdisciplinary research Research that relates to more than one branch of knowledge. It crosses the nominal, artificial boundaries of disciplines or subjects so that knowledge and procedures from more than one discipline can be brought to bear on a problem.

Intersectoral research Research that crosses the nominal, artificial boundaries within society, such as academia, industry, commerce, government, the health and social services sectors, and so on.

Knowledge exchange/transfer The sharing of information, ideas and innovation between the academic sector and a non-academic sector.

Language register The level of formality with which you write, including word usage and tone.

LaTeX A typesetting system designed to produce academic, technical and scientific documentation.

LinkedIn A business and employment-oriented social media site.

Literature review A critique of key themes and an evaluation of important studies within the body of literature and their relevance to a piece of research.

Media relations See **Press office**

Metadata Metadata are the data about data. Your standard data may include facts, statistics, interview notes, textual analysis, and so on. The metadata are the information you use to identify and differentiate these data from other data. Metadata can refer, then, to merely the name of a file, the name of a book, author information, year of publication, and so on.

Methods A 'method' is distinct from 'methodology'. The word 'method' comes from Ancient Greek μέθοδος (méthodos, 'pursuit of knowledge, investigation, mode of prosecuting such inquiry, system'), from μετά (metá, 'after') +ὁδός (hodós, 'way, motion, journey'). As a journey to or pursuit of knowing an object, method is closely tied to epistemology, as in the question and study of knowledge. They are not synonymous, however, as epistemology is more concerned with knowledge in all its respects, whereas method is concerned with how to gain knowledge of something that is already said to exist. In this respect, it is also closely tied to ontology, as in a question of being/reality. **Methodology** is the study of method, usually with a view to justifying the best method for a specific research question.

Milestones   In the context of project planning, an identifiable stage of completion.

Modular   A book required for a teaching course or module.

Monograph   A written piece of work that focuses on one specialised sub-ject with a view to contributing original insight and knowledge. The standard length is anywhere between 60,000 and 80,000 words. Monographs are a com-mon platform for the publication of research in the arts, humanities and social sciences, and tend to result from a culmination of long-term research projects (such as a PhD thesis) and/or smaller research outputs (such as a series of journal publications). Monographs are occasionally published in Science, Technology, Engineering and Mathematics and Medicine (STEMM). STEMM subjects tend to prefer articles over monographs.

Open access   A mechanism by which research outputs are distributed online, free of cost or other barriers.

Open access journal   A journal whose content is open access, often under a Creative Commons Licence allowing free sharing and re-use.

Open access press   A publisher specialising in open access monographs. Some of them using a '**freemium**' model.

Open peer review   A form of peer review of publication for which both authors and peer reviewers are openly known.

Open research   A movement with the aim of making research products, such as publications and datasets, freely available for all to access and use.

ORCID iD   A unique string of numbers that permanently link to your name.

Paradigm   A philosophical and theoretical framework of a scientific school or a discipline within which theories, laws and generalisations and the research methods performed to produce them are formulated.

Peer review   The process of evaluation of a piece of work by fellow scholars, a group of people within your scientific, academic or professional field, charged with maintaining standards. They provide feedback as well as decisions.

Polemic   A use of rhetoric or persuasive writing with the aim of supporting an argument beyond its logical coherence and/or substance. In this respect, a polemic tends to favour poetic and metaphorical expression and the use of emotive expressions.

Predatory journals   The definition is not fully agreed upon currently, but in essence it is any journal whose practices significantly disadvantage the author for the benefit of the publishing company. These may include, but are not limited to, high charges to publish in the journal, active solicitation of articles to be published with little or no peer review quality assurance, or encouraging publication in formats that will have limited circulation and audience reach.

Press office   A university department to support researchers and academics in their interations with the press. It may also be called **Media relations office**.

Principal investigator (PI)   An academic who has secured research funding and is leading a research project, often with research staff working for them.

Quartile One journals   The highest scoring journals on specific impact factors. See also **Four Star journals**.

Reference work   A book concerned primarily with conveying basic information, such as dates, names and terms, e.g. a dictionary on 'Philosophy'. These books are useful for familiarising students with basic information or complex terminology and/or for brushing up on prior knowledge.

Research councils   Government funding bodies for research focused on specific discipline areas. They were formerly grouped together as Research Councils UK (RCUK) but now come under the heading UK Research and Innovation (UKRI).

Research Excellence Framework (REF) UK   A five- to six-yearly UK national ranking of all higher education institutions to determine core funding. Ranking involves peer review of submissions, not simply metrics such as research income, publications, citations, student numbers, the environment and impact. The process was recently reviewed by an independent authority, led by Lord Nicholas Stern: https://www.gov.uk/government/uploads/system/uploads/attachment_data/file/541338/ind-16-9-ref-stern-review.pdf

ResearchGate   A social networking site for scientists and researchers to share papers, ask and answer questions, and find collaborators.

Royalties   Royalties are a form of payment to an author for each copy of a book sold. This is different from an advance, where an author will receive payment upfront, regardless of book sales. Advances are extremely rare where monographs are concerned.

SMART objectives   In the context of project planning, SMART stands for **S**pecific, **M**easurable, **A**ttainable, **R**elevant, **T**ime-bound.

Social media   Websites and applications that enable users to create and share content or to participate in social networking.

Star rating   A rating system from 1* to 4*, with 4* being the highest rating of journal or publication quality.

STEMM   An acronym to represent the disciplines Science, Technology, Engineering, Mathematics and Medicine.

Subscription journal   A journal to which you gain access by paying a membership fee.

Success measures   Specifically-defined targets to enable one to identify if a project or plan has achieved the defined goals.

Summative assessment   See **Assessment, Summative**

Supplementary   Not required, or additional.

Synopsis   A synopsis in this context is a summary of a book, usually provided on the back cover, which is used on websites and leaflets for marketing purposes.

Textbook   A 'textbook' is concerned with surveying the state or history of knowledge in a specific field. These are most commonly used by undergraduate students and are useful in introducing students to a subject of knowledge. They tend to be highly descriptive, with an emphasis on providing fair and balanced accounts of the history and state of research, as opposed to providing novel arguments and interpretations.

Thesis   A written report about a project carried out at masters' level in the USA, for instance, and at doctoral level in the UK, for instance. Also, a proposition or argument.

Third space professionals   University staff who fulfil roles that have academic and administrative aspects yet who fall into neither category but occupy a unique niche as boundaries blur.

Top-tier journals   The journals ranked highest in terms of their citations. See also **Four Star journals** or **Quartile One journals**.

Twitter   A social media site characterised by only allowing short posts.

University press   A publisher associated with and/or run by a university. They therefore tend to be registered as charities. Indeed, their prime interest is in supporting the publication of new research that will contribute to a specific field.

Vanity press   A type of predatory publishing that has low selection criteria and enables little circulation of final product.

Viva voce   An oral examination for an academic qualification. It typically involves the candidate responding to questions about his/her study area and sometimes involves a presentation by the candidate. A closed viva refers to one conducted in private, involving only the candidate, examiners and perhaps a chairperson, and less frequently one observer, say a supervisor or note-taker. An open viva can involve any number of observers.

YouTube   A social media platform for sharing videos.

Index